TIME PIECES

NCQ TITLES

Though each can be read independently,
these NCQ publications, taken together,
comprise a single hyper-text collection.

TIME PIECES

Bernard Sharratt

New Crisis Quarterly
2015

NEW CRISIS QUARTERLY

ncq@newcrisisquarterly.myzen.co.uk

First published 2015

ISBN : 978-1-910956-06-9

For Pauline
who has known me
all my time

CONTENTS

FOREWORD

The present book re-prints three linked essays which have appeared previously, but originally in rather different times and contexts. The first was published, thanks to David Punter, in a collection entitled *Introduction to Contemporary Cultural Sudies* (1986), and was a preliminary and mildly performative attempt to sketch out some of the issues around time which have since continued to preoccupy me. It could be up-dated with more recent data, but the core issues remain, as ever, the same. The second took the form of a review of an imagined work which, as with all the reviews in my *The Literary Labyrinth* (1984), was of a book I didn't then feel I had the time actually to write. The third was written in a somewhat concentrated two days back in 1985, as a rushed contribution to an then-imminent collection of essays on Derrida, to be edited by Martin Stanton, but which never appeared: it takes the form of a lengthy critique of a short essay by Derrida on a brief footnote in Heidegger. This perhaps rather esoteric piece had a *samizdat* existence for a few decades, in an increasingly tattered typescript and in variously distributed photocopies, and was finally and digitally resuscitated by an old friend, Venkat Rao, for a volume published in India in 2009 entitled *Theory After Derrida*. It may have a continuing relevance for some readers, and amuse others.

One day, I thought, I would actually write the work on how once-emerging technologies might foster the kind of time-saving and potentially revolutionary changes in material production—for use rather than for exchange—which I proleptically indicated in the imagined review, and I am pleased to see that very recent technologies, such as home-based 3D printing, now make that future programme ever more realisable than before. And I also once thought that I might follow through the critique of Derrida with a full and positive account of why I believe there can be a properly materialist account of time.

Since I am now finally retired from other commitments and from the usual academic constraints, I might be thought to have time enough, and no excuse for not actually writing those once-imagined books. Well, I plead arthritis in my writing hand. And other ailments of increasing age. Or the lure of several other books I still want to write, instead. Or a sense that, at least as a preliminary exercise, in this new era of blogs, e-readers, self-publishing, and print on demand, I might in any case re-cycle my own previous work, as everybody else does, provided not too many trees are sacrificed. Or a growing sense that some of my once out-of-date concerns are again sharply relevant in our current crises. Or any other reasons or excuses you prefer to provide. For now.

Yet time remains, obviously, a current issue for me, though the apparent nature of the issue perhaps changes, from Augustine to Einstein, and indeed before and after them, in Aristotle or Dirac, Heraclitus or Debord. So, as a temporary expedient, I have at least revived, as my self-publishing imprint, 'New Crisis Quarterly', the title of the extremely short-lived journal whose first, only, and valedictory issue appeared in May 1984, under the guise of *The Literary Labyrinth*. It was the editorial policy of that defunct periodical not only to publish reviews of imaginary works by fictive authors but also to invite its readers actually to write the works reviewed, if they felt so inclined.

My readers therefore, as in the past, are now, and again, encouraged to consider whether they feel inclined actually to complete the pieces they are about to read. There admittedly remains a lingering nostalgia about the very exercise of reviving such long-deceased occasional pieces. But it's a short book, and shouldn't take too much time to read.

B.S.
2015

TOWARDS THE CULTURAL STUDY OF TIME

This essay attempts little more than to outline the shadow of a concept, a possible object of inquiry, a notion that in a puzzling way already haunts a great deal of 'contemporary cultural studies' yet is rarely the explicit centre of attention or research. Its focus is that difficult and slippery term: time. My approach is to begin from the apparently obvious in order to suggest the increasingly complex problems concealed by that obviousness. The structure of the essay is, however, mosaic rather than linear, offering materials for consideration and discussion rather than any overall argument or thesis.

1: Timing activities

Consider the following statistical statements, summaries and tables:

Cinema attendances reached a peak in 1946 (when one third of the population were going once a week, 13 per cent twice a week).

The number of viewing-hours had risen fairly sharply at the end of the sixties, but held steady, with perhaps a very slight increase, in the seventies. In the 1977-79 period, average hours viewed per week were sixteen in the summer and twenty in the winter . . The average number of hours listened to per week in 1978/9 was about nine hours.

In America, the normal working year consists of 1,976 hours against an average of 2,137 hours in Britain.

In 1968 manual employees in industry worked on average just over 46 hours per week . . In her study of managers Stewart found that the average working week lasted for 42½ hours; . . and in his investigation Copeman found heads of department averaging 41¼ hours per week whilst managing directors had a somewhat more arduous time with a typical working week of 49½ hours.

. . a Gallup Poll survey in Britain in 1964 found that one out of six male workers had a spare-time job taking up an average of twelve hours per week.

. . only 6 per cent of those earning under £650 p.a. have three weeks or more paid leave compared with 44 per cent of those earning £1,950 and over.

Proportion of Leisure Time Spent on Different Activities 1969 (percentages)

Activity	All males	All females
Television	23	23
Reading	5	9
Crafts and hobbies	4	17
Decorating & House-maintenance	8	1
Gardening	12	7
Social activities	3	9
Drinking	3	1
Cinema and theatre	1	1

One could easily multiply examples of these familiar forms of comment upon or summarizations of various relations between time and activity.[1] An influential sub-branch of statistical sociology has even emerged under the label 'time-budget studies'. In the introduction to the published report of the most ambitious multinational comparative time-budget survey, Alexander Szalai writes:[2]

This conventional name has some metaphoric justification, since very many studies of this kind are concerned primarily with the proportions in which the twenty-four hours of the day are allocated the various activities by people belonging to certain groups or strata of the population—how many hours and

[1] The quotations above are from: Marwick, *British Society since 1945*, p. 75; Marwick, p. 250; Kenneth Roberts, *Leisure*, Longmans 1970, p. 10; Roberts, p. 21 (twice); *Trends in British Society since 1900*, ed. A. H. Halsey, Macmillan 1972, p. 541; ed. Halsey, p. 553. I am grateful to Hugh Cunningham, Steve Hipkin, Ray Pahl, Dave Reason and Kevin Robins for bibliographical and other suggestions during the writing of this essay, which was completed in 1983. Some of the themes are pursued further in my *The Literary Labyrinth,* Harvester 1984.
[2] *The Use of Time,* ed A. Szalai, Mouton, The Hague 1972, p. 1.

minutes such people spend daily on chores and pastimes such as doing work, putting things straight in the household, shopping around, taking meals, visiting friends, reading books, listening to the radio, having a good night's rest, and so forth. This type of investigation is indeed somewhat similar to the procedure by which the allocation of funds for different purposes in financial budgets is analysed. As far as personal or family budgets are concerned, the similarity will even extend to many specific types of expenditure, because a great number of everyday activities involve not alone the expenditure of time but of money as well. At this point however, the resemblance comes to an end. Time can only be spent, not 'earned'. Therefore time-budgets have no income side. The fund of time which is being 'allocated' to various activities (24 hours in daily time-budgets, 7 x 24 hours in weekly time-budgets, etc.) serves simply as a frame of reference for setting out the temporal proportions of people's engagement in the whole gamut of their daily activities. Thus, it is not time itself, either as a physical or as a subjectively perceived entity, but rather as the use people make of their time, which is the real subject of time-budget studies.

If, however, the 'use' of time is the subject of such studies, one could perhaps ask: what, then, is actually being 'measured' when the results are put in statistical or percentage form? As the conclusion to one of the studies in that same report comments:[3]

> From the viewpoint of biology if breathing is normal, its duration is insignificant; but if it stops the difference between one and ten minutes is fatal for man. If one goes without sleep for one night no serious consequences will ensue, yet over a longer period of time a minimum of sleep expressed in hours and minutes per day is necessary for man's existence, health and well-being.
>
> Similarly, from the point of view of economics 20 hours of shopping can be taken as merely an indicator of the decision to purchase which again is nothing but a point in time, thus has no dimension in time even though it might as a process have taken one minute or one month.

---

[3] Katja Boh and Stane Saksida, 'An attempt at a typology of time use', in ed. Szalai, p. 245.

From the point of view of the sociological content and significance of an activity it can be seen that both a worker and a manager can work ten hours daily, but this fact can be utilised in only a limited number of very specific theories. By and large this fact is theoretically often irrelevant.

Yet the potential significance of precisely this curious 'irrelevance' for any theoretically-informed 'cultural studies' seems considerable—if only because a preoccupation with the 'use' of time has deeply shaped one of the major influences upon cultural studies: Marxist theory.

2: Marxism and time

In the foreword to the English translation of Marx's *Herr Vogt* the editors write:

> *Herr Vogt* is Marx's 'forgotten' work. Mentioned in passing—if at all—in biographical studies, and scarcely at all in discussions of his writings, it has remained for over a century largely neglected.
>   Yet this is the work which Marx took the best part of a year away from the writing of *Capital to* complete. It is an answer to the slanders against himself, Engels and their supporters which appeared in Karl Vogt's 1859 pamphlet, *Mem Prozess gegen die Allgemeine Zeitung.* He knew before its publication that many 'clever men' would be 'completely unable to grasp how I could squander my time on refuting such infantile nonsense'.[4]

Capital itself is concerned, at various points in its argument, with a variety of 'times'—circulation time, time of production, time of consumption, buying and selling time, capital turnover time, etc. —but at the core of its analysis of capitalism are a number of interlinked concepts, among which a certain conceptualisation of time is crucial.

Marx's analysis begins from a distinction between 'use-value' and 'exchange-value' and he advances the argument that the

---

[4] Karl Marx, *Herr Vogt,* trans. R. A. Archer, New Park Publications, New York 1982, p. ix.

ultimate basis of exchange-value is 'socially necessary labour time', which fundamentally underpins the dynamics of capitalist production and capitalist exploitation. Two factors are central.

First, and in its simplest formulation, exploitation is conceived in terms of the difference between, on the one hand, the length of the working day during which the worker's labour-power produces the value of the wage paid to the worker and, on the other, the 'additional' length of the working day during which the worker produces a further (surplus) value from which the capitalist's profit is derived, but for which the worker receives no wage, no 'exchange-value' in return for the 'use-value' of his labour-power. This simple analysis can, obviously, be modified and developed into a far more complex analysis (in terms, for example, of relative and absolute surplus value) but its core argument still appeals to a notion of capitalist control over the use of workers' labour-power for a certain time.

Secondly, and as part of that more complex analysis, the differences between the rates of profit of competing capitalist concerns can ultimately be analysed in terms of the relation between the amounts of labour time actually utilized in production and the 'socially necessary' labour time currently required for such production; this line of analysis would take in such factors as the relation between 'fixed' and 'variable capital', the 'rate of exploitation', the adoption or otherwise of technological innovation, etc.

The most explicit political implication of this two-fold analysis, within Marx's own argument, is that the decisive struggle within capitalism is engaged over control of labour-power during the process of production. Again at its simplest, this can be a struggle over the length of the working day itself (as in Marx's own vivid account) or in more complicated forms over such issues as productivity, piece-rates, and the speeding-up of production processes— all of which focus ultimately on relations between work and time. It is these conflicts which are fundamental, if not of themselves decisive, in the relations between labour and capital and between competing capitalists.

5

Yet a less obvious struggle over time is also involved, which has been brilliantly explored by E. P. Thompson: the struggle over the relationship to and very conception of 'time' which is dominant in our daily lives.[5] In a long process, a particular and historically specific notion of time was inculcated and imposed in the general development of capitalism. Towards the end of his lengthy analysis Thompson writes: 'In all these ways—by the division of labour; the supervision of labour; fines; bells and clocks; money incentives; preachings and schoolings; the suppression of fairs and sports—new labour habits were formed and a new time-discipline was imposed. '[6]

One could summarize that shift in 'time-sense' and change in 'the inward apprehension of time' in the notion not only that 'time is money' but that time is *like* money: a matter of equal quantifiable units. As Thompson remarks: 'Time is now currency: it is not passed but spent.' From that it is a very short step to 'time-budget studies', in which, however 'Time can only be spent, not earned'.

There is, however, a further aspect of Marx's analysis which is more difficult to conceptualise. If one asks what is to replace capitalism and with it perhaps those now correlative notions of time and money, Marx's own answers are, at a certain level, problematic. His best-known formulation of communist daily life comes from *The German Ideology:*

. . in communist society, where nobody has one exclusive sphere of activity but each can become accomplished in any

---

[5] See E. P. Thompson, 'Time, work-discipline and industrial capitalism'. *Past and Present,* No. 38 (1967), pp. 56-97. Cf. also Nigel Thrift, 'Owners' Time and Own Time: the making of a capitalist time consciousness, 1300-1880', in *Space and Time in Geography,* ed. A. Pred, Gleerup, Lund 1981, pp. 56-84. Michel Foucault's discussion of discipline in schools is also relevant, in his *Discipline and Punish.* See also the recent historical survey by David S. Landes, *Revolution in Time: Clocks and the Making of the Modern World,* Belknap Press, Harvard University Press, Cambridge, Mass. 1984; and André Gorz, 'Towards a Politics of Time', in *Farewell to the Working Class,* Pluto 1982.
[6] Thompson, p. 90.

branch he wishes, society regulates the general production and thus makes it possible for me to do one thing today and another tomorrow, to hunt in the morning, fish in the afternoon, rear cattle in the evening, criticize after dinner, just as I have a mind to, without ever becoming hunter, fisherman, shepherd or critic.[7]

Lest one should be tempted to assimilate this account to a time-budget analysis of part-time activities and full-time work, or presume a distinction between 'professional' and 'amateur' activities, it is worth quoting a less well-known passage from the same work[8]:

> with a communist organisation, there disappears ... the subordination of the artist to some definite art, thanks to which he is exclusively a painter, sculptor, etc. . . In a communist society there are no painters but at most people who engage in painting among other activities.

The implications of this conception for modes of 'social organization' are very far-reaching indeed, as G. A. Cohen has pointed out.[9]

Nevertheless, there remains a constant emphasis in Marx's thinking upon the overall reduction of 'socially necessary' labour-time, that deployment of time required to produce the 'necessities' of social life ('society regulates the general production'), and therefore to some extent a continuing practical distinction between what would now be characterized as 'work' and as 'leisure' or 'free time'.

An alternative emphasis within the Marxist tradition can, of course, be traced, upon the reconstruction of 'work' as itself to be characterized by the qualities we now associate with such 'leisure' notions as creativity, self-realization, enjoyment—an emphasis most forcefully registered in William Morris, and sharply in contrast to some

---

[7] Marx and Engels, *The German Ideology*, pp. 44-5.
[8] Marx and Engels, *The German Ideology*, p. 432.
[9] G. A. Cohen, *Karl Marx's Theory of History: a defence*. Clarendon Press 1978, p. 133.

conventional assumptions in current categorizations of 'leisure' and 'work'.[10]

Yet there remains a further, and even more intractable, conceptual distinction still operative in Marx's thought: that between use-value and exchange-value. If capitalism is premissed upon production for exchange-value, then communism will be predicated upon production for 'use' even if some mode of distribution of 'use-values' is necessary, albeit not governed by 'exchange-values'. Yet the notion of concrete use (-value) is not assimilable to any conceptualisation of 'abstract' labour or therefore of 'abstract' time. At its simplest, there is no commensurability between 'use'-times as there may be, at a certain level of analysis, between 'production'-times. Implicit therefore in any Marxist notion of a post-capitalist mode of life is— however proleptically—a non-capitalist conceptualisation of time, or at least the construction of a historically specific 'time-sense' and 'inward apprehension of time' different from that which has been constructed in the development of capitalism.

Given the formidable difficulties of attempting to anticipate any such fundamental re-conceptualisation, what follows can at best be a series of tentative suggestions, the first of which concerns the relevance of some of these considerations to 'contemporary cultural studies'. As will become clear, the suggestion also takes, in fact, the form of an oblique experiment.

3: Cultural Studies, Marxism, Semiotics, Psychoanalysis

The various attempts to engender a programme of 'contemporary cultural studies' under the aegis of a putatively Marxist approach have tended to retain, through many reformulations and theoretical redirections, a working

---

[10] Cf. the discussion of the mutually exclusive categories of 'remunerated work' and 'activities oriented towards self-fulfilment' in Joffre Dumazedier, *Sociology of Leisure*, trans. M. A. McKenzie, Elsevier, Amsterdam 1974, p. 67ff.

distinction between 'levels' of analysis, whether in such traditional terms as base/superstructure or in various revamped terminologies (e.g., the economic, political and ideological 'instances' of a social formation), but even when the several reformulations have yielded a recognition of the 'relative autonomy' of the objects of study defined as 'cultural', the allegiance to Marxism has been most deeply registered in the emphasis on the concept or metaphor of 'production'.

As with the classical Marxist critique of political economy, any consideration of 'consumption' has been conceptually subordinated to analysis of the processes of production, a subordination which is itself an inner premise of the more general theoretical formulae. Thus, even in relation to the relatively autonomous instances or domains, the angle of analysis has characteristically been upon the 'production of meanings' and upon modes of control over that production.

In the allied and overlapping fields of literary, film and media studies, the primary concern has been the apparatuses of 'textual' production, for example in terms of the 'positioning' of the reader-spectator. Even in the reluctant encounter between Marxist literary theory and reader-response approaches, the difficulty of reconciling the site of production with the site of reception and response has been acute, visible in the predominant emphasis upon the construction of sites of reception internal to (implied in) the production process, the operation of the 'text'. There is an obvious continuity throughout these Marxist approaches with such familiar political concerns as the 'control' and 'ownership' of the 'means of production', a recognition or definition of that as the decisive terrain of power.

Yet some awkward problems have always hovered over this characteristic Marxist preoccupation—or, more strictly perhaps, have fallen outside the specific conceptual reach of Marxism. The concepts of 'use-value' and 'need' have remained, almost as it were of necessity, relegated to a merely contingent and 'concrete' specification, often

9

assigned to the conceptually barren level of the 'individual'. The recognition of 'concrete' labour has been correspondingly cursory.

In his repudiation of any methodological individualism Marx was pursuing a political as well as an intellectual trajectory: socialism was allied to forms of collectivity and solidarity as against 'private' modes of appropriation and competition, and the countervailing power to that of private capital had to be the construction of a proletarian class and class-interest.

Obviously, certain alleged lacunae within this schema could then be focussed on: the role of the individual in history (not least Marx himself) or the problem of personal commitment and choice (class allegiance). But an undeniable perplexity remained endemic to the schema itself: if socialism-communism was to be characterized by production for use rather than exchange, 'from each according to his ability, to each according to his needs', then the conceptually unelaborated notions of use-value, need, and concrete labour (all of which seemed to involve specification at the 'level' of the 'individual') were intrinsic to any positive, rather than simply reactive, conception of countervailing class-interest. Almost by its own definitions, therefore, the Marxist analysis of capitalism was unable, and not simply reluctant, to generate a coherent conceptualisation of socialism.

It is worth sketching some partial parallels to these problems within two other major influences upon recent cultural analysis: semiotics and psychoanalysis. Saussure's founding gesture of modem linguistics, which underpins later semiological approaches, was to distinguish *langue* from *parole* in order to constitute the former as methodological object. Yet the conceptual subordination (or even theoretical expulsion) of *parole* and the emphasis upon the systemic arbitrariness (un-motivatedness) of the relation between signifier and signified left open not only the problems of historical change (diachronic linguistics) and 'semantics' but also the problem of transgressive or 'creative' language and in particular the problem of 'trying to mean'—that reaching beyond the resources of an available combinatory that is endemic to actual language-use and exchange.

Recent interest in the emphasis of Bakhtin-Volosinov upon the 'dialogic' and 'multi-accentual' character of language indicates a move to recovery of a perspective from which these issues might be rethought, and with them the conceptual status of the individual, concrete 'speech-act' which structural linguistics left inadequately explored. Saussure himself, in distinguishing the syntagmatic axis from the 'associative' axis, arguably retained more awareness of the multi-accentual than later formulations in terms of the 'paradigmatic', and it may well be through a return to Saussure's wider notion of the associative, including individual 'associations',[11] that a firmer bridge to psychoanalysis could be sought.

The assimilation of psychoanalysis in cultural studies has also been shadowed by a similar (and perhaps less justified) conceptual subordination of the 'concrete' to the systemic. The problem of methodological individualism is acute in Freud's own work, in the interaction between particular case-studies and theoretical elaboration, but in classic psychoanalytic practice the necessary focus has to be upon the individual analysand in a specific transference-situation with an analyst. Divorced from that (dialogic) interaction any 'application' of psychoanalytic procedures or even concepts becomes vulnerable to a peculiar vacuity. Yet even within the collaborative construction and articulation of the particular analysis there are endemic perplexities, registered in Freud's recognition of the potential 'interminability' of any analysis and (correspondingly) the difficulty of any coherent conceptualisation of 'cure'. Lacan's notion of the necessary irreducibility of *désir to* full articulation is in part a reformulation of this problem.

These compressed comments do not entail any simple rejection of the methodological premisses of Marxism, semiotics or psychoanalysis, in their various emphases upon

---

[11] F. de Saussure, *Course in General Linguistics,* trans. W. Baskin, Fontana, 1974, pp. 125-7.

the structural, synchronic and systemic, but are indicative of certain internal conceptual limits which are the necessary obverse of those premises. That a certain dissatisfaction with such approaches has emerged within cultural studies for other reasons (leading for example to a re-prioritization of the 'experiential', whether in feminist inquiries or ethnological methods) is not my concern here. Rather, I want to outline some major problems within cultural studies which perhaps echo the difficulties I have indicated.

It is clear that an important impetus behind the development of cultural studies was the project or promise of locating, articulating and analysing a countervailing force against capitalism, whether in terms of opposing collective-communal values or residual-emergent cultural resistances. Variations of this optimism found formulation in such notions as counter-culture and hegemonic struggle. Yet the characteristic tone of cultural analysis has been deeply ambivalent, a complex awareness of incorporation-resilience (to use an early vocabulary for this recognition). Arguably the problem registered here is precisely that of conceptualising 'post-capitalist' needs, demands and desires, of formulating what reaches beyond an available system of articulation, of what are to count as the constituents of the projected 'cure'.

Another early impetus had been the questioning of a received dichotomization of 'cultural value', that between 'high' and 'low', elite and mass 'culture', posed most often in terms of judgements directed at artifacts but applying more generally to 'ways of living'. Yet here too a certain ambivalence is traceable, not only in implicit re-discriminations across received boundaries but more paradoxically in the utilization of a formidable intellectual armoury drawn undeniably from the 'highest' resources of 'bourgeois culture', an affirmation in itself of a certain conception of countervailing resources available 'within' capitalism. Yet such a recognition reinforces awareness precisely of the (linked) problems of individual allegiance-commitment and of the peculiar specificity and differentiation of cultural artifacts and processes, not only in their production and composition but in the concrete and 'individual' *use* made of them. It is this latter aspect that I now want to highlight.

4: *Questions and quotations*

I should now make it plain that the preceding Sections 2 and 3 of this essay have been written not solely as exposition but also as a kind of experiment, an attempt, upon the reader. I can therefore now put a series of grouped questions concerning time to that reader—i.e., to you, the specific, gendered, class-located individual of a certain age and ethnic identity currently reading this page.

What kind of sense, if any, does it make to ask *how long* you took to *read* sections 2 and 3 of this essay? If one tried to answer the question 'how long? ' in terms of minutes, would what is measured by those minutes be the same whether you had understood what you were reading or not? Could one sensibly ask how long it took you to *understand* (or partially understand, or not understand) those sections? Would an answer to that question involve assessing the 'duration' of your previous reading of Marxism, semiotics, psychoanalysis? Would it also involve calculating 'how long' it took you to learn how to read? Or to 'learn' English? And would these various 'durations' be in any sense additional or cumulative with respect to each other?

If section 3 was recognized as in part a re-working of some of the contents of section 2, does this imply that section 3 could, or even should, be read more quickly than section 2, or understood more quickly? Does it make sense to ask 'how much' of section 3 was a repetition or recurrence of section 2?

In what sense, if any, might reading these sections have 'saved' or 'wasted' time for you? When we read a footnoted reference to a work we haven't read, does this imply a potential 'multiplier effect' on our reading? Does it take as long to understand a précis of *Capital* as it does to understand *Capital?*

Does it make any sense to ask how long it took me to *write* those sections? If Marx had not written *Herr Vogt* what kind of implications might that have had for the time he took to write *Capital?*

Moreover, in what contexts would it make sense to seek to compare (how?) the time taken by different individuals to read sections 2 and 3? For example, would it take you longer to type a manuscript that you understood than one you did not?

Bearing in mind the table cited earlier, for example, can these questions be adapted to ask about watching a television programme, attending a play, listening to a piece of music, watching a film—and what difference does it make that it is plausible in all these cases to assign a 'stop-watch' timing to the 'performance' that is invariable by an individual in the audience? How far could such questions be extended to cultural activities which are not so bounded by explicit performance limits—such as reading?

Many more questions along these lines could certainly be formulated, though I would suggest that the two most basic that would eventually emerge would be an epistemological question and a political question: first, is the sense of a question determined by the possibility of its being answered, and, second, in what senses could the division of labour between manual and mental labour be overcome? Involved in both questions, perhaps, is a further question, concerning the *use* you can or intend to make of (the time passed reading) this collection of essays.

Rather than pursue these questions directly, however, I now want to offer a series of quotations which I think have a bearing upon the problems I am trying in various ways to bring into focus:

1830-1840 :

Read asked: 'How much should be allowed as the wage of the "owner of capital" superintending the industrious undertaking?' John Rae answered that the profit of stock must include a return for the mental exertion and anxiety of

14

the owner of stock. J. S. Mill argued that such a wage was not determined in the same way as other wages, but was a commission on capital employed. And Ramsay went yet further, by distinguishing the function of supervisor and entrepreneur from that of the capitalist. The entrepreneur did not do manual labour, and his profits could not be said to be proportional to his 'mental qualities 'as these could not be quantified . . The level of payment for these qualities of entrepreneurship and abstinence was expected to be determined by social criteria. Returns, argued Scrope, were to be sufficient to pay the ordinary rate of profit on total capital, 'as well as remunerate him for his skill and trouble, according to the standard of remunerations generally expected by his class'. [12]

1983 :

. . we have taken the advice of an eminent barrister, and, while it is a nice point and has not yet been argued in the higher courts, he thinks that the election might stand provided that I became a fugitive from the kingdom. He was very attentive to us, and gave us a full seven minutes of his advice, and he charged for his counsel only £800. [13]

1830-1835 :

Fees or Charges for Chemical Analysis or for Business Relative to the Application of Science to the Arts and Manufacturers. Consultation:
Written opinion on a short case or letter of inquiry.
Fee £2.2.0
For a series of chemical experiments per day.
Fee £5.5.0

---

[12] Maxine Berg, *The Machinery Question and the Making of Political Economy 1815-1848,* Cambridge University Press 1980, pp. 123-4.
[13] E. P. Thompson, *The Defence of Britain,* CND 1983, p. 35.

Attendance in London to view any manufactory; to examine apparatus or inspect any chemical process.
Fee £4.4.0
For similar attendance which shall occupy the whole or chief part of the day
Fee £6.6.0
Attendance at a distance from London exclusive of travelling expenses per day. *Fee £7.7.0* [14]

1878: Trial of Whistler :

—'A stiffish price', suggested the Attorney-General, 'two hundred guineas. How soon did you "knock it off"? '
—'As well as I remember, about a day . . I may still have put a few more touches to it the next day if the painting were not dry. I had better say, then, that I was two days at work on it. '
—'The labour of two days then is that for which you ask two hundred guineas?'
—'No. I ask it for the knowledge of a lifetime.' [15]

1874: Letter from William Morris :

Monday was a day here to set one longing to get away: as warm as June . . though town looks rather shocking on such days, and then instead of the sweet scents one gets an extra smell of dirt. Surely if people lived five hundred years instead of threescore and ten they would find some better way of living than in such a sordid loathsome place, but now it seems to be nobody's business to try to better things— isn't mine you see in spite of all my grumbling . . [16]

[14] Quoted in Berg, p. 198.
[15] Adapted from William Gaunt, *The Aesthetic Adventure,* Cape 1975, p. 90.
[16] Quoted in E. P. Thompson, *William Morris: romantic to revolutionary,* Merlin 1977, p. 194.

It is absolutely impossible to understand how he found time for all his activities, at the same time keeping some supervision over the Firm, and (before the end of 1886) launching on a translation of Homer. In these two years he wrote *The Pilgrims of Hope, A Dream of John Ball,* and the first part of *Socialism from the Root Up*: articles, notes and editorials for *Commonweal* : he delivered something like 120 lectures, about fifteen of which (at the least) were written out in long-hand and are permanent contributions to Socialist theory: he attended the weekly Executive Council meetings of the League, the Ways and Means Committee, and goodness knows how many other meetings besides: he made tours of the provinces, breaking new ground, and consolidating old branches—Dublin, Scotland, Yorkshire and Lancashire, the Potteries, East Anglia and a dozen other centres. He was present at sixty out of the ninety-nine meetings of the Committee of the Hammersmith Branch, at some of which only two or three others troubled to attend: and in addition was often in the Chair at the Sunday evening lectures—if he was not lecturing elsewhere himself. He spoke at scores of open-air meetings, chaired them, carried the banner, sold literature, took round the hat for collections. He acted as a sandwichman, between placards advertising *Commonweal.* He gave a hand with the smallest mechanical details of office or branch organisation, and wrote basketfuls of correspondence. He edited *Commonweal.* He attended the police-courts. He drew up balance-sheets, and subsidized the movement with his money. He helped with social evenings, gave readings of his own work or wrote special poems, entertained speakers, and made personal contacts with people sympathetic to the movement . . Successive biographers have lamented this 'waste' of Morris's energies.[17]

---

[17] Thompson, *William Morris*, pp. 423-4.

1978 :

He was pondering the first three bits. Suddenly, without thinking about it, he was drawing another box below the first box . . The segment number—the area code—would be the same as the ring number, which defined the level of security to which the compartment would be assigned. Three bits can be combined in eight different ways. So there would be eight rings (eight levels of security) and eight segments (eight area codes) in the memory system. The area codes themselves would indicate which ring was forbidden to whom. . . . . Although they are generally shy about claiming to have had one, engineers often speak of 'the golden moment' in order to describe the feeling—it comes rarely enough—when the scales fall from a designer's eyes and a problem's right solution is suddenly there . . As for Wallach, after he had drawn the diagram, he stared at it, wondering for a moment, 'Where did that come from?'[18]

Early 1970s :

The Eclipse was to be Data General's first microcoded machine. Alsing signed up for the job . . . and then he procrastinated. Month after month, his boss would ask him how the code was coming along and he would say: 'Fine. A few problems, but pretty well.' In fact, though, he had not written a single line of code. Finally, he could sense that his boss and some of his colleagues were growing angry; failure had become an almost palpable object —a pair of headlights coming towards him down the wrong side of a road. Scared, he packed up the necessary circuit diagrams, specs and manuals and went to the Boston Public Library . . The Eclipse contained 195 assembly-language instructions, which in the end Alsing encoded in some 390 micro-instructions, many of which performed multiple duties. He said he wrote most of those micro-instructions in two weeks at the library.

---

[18] Tracy Kidder, *The Soul of a New Machine,* Penguin 1982, p. 77.

Perhaps it really took him less; West believed that Alsing did it all in two days and nights. 'Without question he did,' West insisted.[19]

1979 :

There's a clock inside Eagle. It ticks every 220 billionths of a second. Between each tick of the clock. Eagle performs one microinstruction.[20]

1970 :

The rate-fixers cannot but set a production time which demands a superhuman effort, since the whole point of the norms is to hold wages down to a level fixed in advance. If, for example, the sum of 61 forints has been fixed as the wage for a day's work at one hundred per cent performance, the rate-fixers are obliged to set the time per piece so that a minute of work does not yield more than the level fixed for the category; that is, the wage for a full minute's work. Even if the workers don't think like this, the rate-fixers are doing so all the time. Their point of departure is the pay itself—the 'incentive' of a danger to one's living standards—and not their experience of the true time taken to make a piece. Their stop-watches give a result which has been determined in advance, and this is the reason why the allocated times per piece, with very few exceptions, are unrealisable.[21]

*

Most of these quotations concern what we would probably classify as 'work-time', yet particularly insofar as they involve 'mental' labour (as reading this essay does) they highlight the difficulty of assimilating production time to any measure of homogenous units.

---

[19] Kidder, p. 94.
[20] Kidder, p. 116.
[21] Miklos Haraszti, *A Worker in a Worker's State,* trans. M. Wright, Penguin 1977, p. 40.

One could add further quotations to do with such activities as teaching, nursing, counselling, child-rearing, etc., yet I would suggest that our habitual way of considering and, more crucially, of organizing even these activities in their character as socially-defined 'work' often tries to align them with a dominant time-awareness that is at odds with their specific, concrete, character.

5: Time and Cultural Studies

Pursuing the mosaic patterning of this essay, I now want to indicate ways in which the problem of 'cultural time' already lurks within some of the preoccupations, and the possible intellectual resources, of cultural studies—not least in that ambivalent qualifier 'contemporary'.

That 'time' has been a concern within a variety of disciplines is apparent. Both Anglo-American and continental philosophers have devoted considerable recent work to the problem of time.[22] Modernist literature has produced a rich exploration, in Joyce's *Ulysses*, Proust's *À la recherche du temps perdu*, Eliot's *Four Quartets*, Butor's *L'emploi du temps*. Science Fiction writing has sometimes shown a more complex awareness of 'time' problems than those of mere time-travel.[23] Post-Einstein physics, the *Annales* historians, the Lund school of time-geography, cognitive theory and developmental psychology, anthropology and ethnography, and of course economics, have all broached the problems of 'time' as variously defined by those disciplines, and it would be an intriguing task in itself to

[22] See, e.g.. *The Philosophy of Time,* ed. R. M. Gale, Harvester 1978; Hugh Mellor, *Real Time,* Cambridge University Press 1980; Edmund Husserl, *The Phenomenology of Internal Time-Consciousness,* trans. J. S. Churchill, Martinus Nijhoff, The Hague 1964; Martin Heidegger, *Being and Time,* trans. J. Macquarrie and E. Robinson, Harper and Row, New York 1962; Derrida, 'Ousia and Grammè', in *Phenomenology in Perspective,* ed. F. J. Smith, Martinus Nijhoff, The Hague 1970, pp. 54-93.

[23] See, for example, the use made of a galactic perspective upon earth's history in Lessing's *Canopus in Argos: Archives.*

trace the cultural significance, and percolated impact, of such intellectual concerns.[24]

Yet cultural studies have rarely focussed directly upon the contemporary cultural construction of time-sense and time-awareness or upon the current social organization of time. In a tentative way notions of 'generational' group identification and of individual biographical trajectory have been deployed in specific studies, and occasionally a particular inquiry yields intriguing material. Some instances can be very briefly commented upon, from work done at the Birmingham Centre for Contemporary Cultural Studies.

Dorothy Hobson, in her 'Housewives and the mass media',[25] points out that 'In some cases switching on the radio is part of the routine of beginning the day; it is, in fact, the first *boundary* in the working day. In terms of the 'structurelessness' of the experience of housework the time boundaries provided by radio are important in the women's own division of their time.' As Hobson also points out, the constant time-checks on radio and the time-referring programme titles *(The Breakfast Show, Mid-Morning Programme, The World at One)* help to structure the daily work-sequence. Some comments quoted in her study suggest a particular time-awareness linking across days:

---

[24] See, for example: F. Braudel, *The Mediterranean and the Mediterranean World in the Age of Philip II* (2 vols.), trans. S. Reynolds, Coffins 1972-3; Ernest Labrousse, *Esquisse du mouvement des prix et des revenus en France au XVIIIe siecle*, Dalioz, Paris 1933; Pred, 'The choreography of existence: comments on Hagerstrand's time-geography and its usefulness', *Economic Geography*, No. 53 (1977), pp. 207-21; Pred, 'Production, family, and free-time projects: a time-geographic perspective on the individual and societal change in nineteenth-century US cities'. *Journal of Historical Geography*, VII, 1 (1981), 3-36; *The Developmental Psychology of Time*, ed. W. J. Friedman, Academic Press 1982.

[25] D. Hobson, 'Housewives and the mass media', in *Culture, Media, Language*, eds. Stuart Hall et al., pp. 104-14.

Q: What do you like about the programmes that you watch?
A: Something to look forward to the next day 'cos most of them are serials.

And:

Q: Why do you like *Crossroads?*
A: Just that you like to know what happens next, you know. I mean they're terrible actors, I know that, and I just see through that, you know.

The response introducing this comment on *Crossroads* is itself interesting:

. . in between half-five and eight, that's me busiest time, feed him, change him, sometimes bath him. I don't bath him very often, erm, get Richard's dinner and I always clean up straight away, the washing up, and then I get everything settled and that takes me up to 8 o'clock, 'cos I stop at half-past-six to watch *Crossroads [laughs].* And then from 8 onwards I just sit and watch the box *[laughs].*

One would need, of course, a great deal more to go on, but—and especially insofar as this pattern is also recognizable within one's own life—even these pointers suggest the potential usefulness of such notions as 'boundaries', time-embedding ('cos I stop at half-past-six'), time-deepening (simultaneity of activities), temporal matching (parallel sequences of activities), temporal horizons (something to look forward to next day, next week, etc.), displaced and suspended overlapping temporalities (the various serial narratives each pursuing their own rhythms yet intersecting with one's own daily routines, the different levels of regularity inflecting each other), and perhaps most importantly the overarching notion of recurrence rather than repetition (one might think here of differences between childcare, housework, and industrial production-line work).[26]

---

[26] For the distinction between 'repetition' and 'recurrence', see David Reason, 'Classification, Time and the Organisation of Production', in

One might attempt to develop and apply such notions to a time-sense operating upon, or perhaps being reproduced at the level of, a different temporal span (for example, a 'marriage' as a latent temporal category) and one could probably compare the time-sense, time-organization and horizons operative in 'housework' and in 'political' awareness and activities: their respective necessities and the congruence or incompatibilities between them. It is also arguable that 'being a housewife' involves a degree of necessary dissociation from the time-discipline Thompson has analysed as constructed within capitalist development. Socially as well as biologically constructed gender differences in 'inward apprehension of time' may sometimes be an important basis of conflict and incomprehension.

Paul Corrigan's 'Doing Nothing',[27] an excerpt from his study of Sunderland street-corner culture," suggests other directions of inquiry:

- What sort of things do you do with your mates?
- *Duncan:* Just stand around talking about footy. About things.
- Do you do anything else?
- *Duncan:* Joke, lark about, carry on. Just what we feel like really.
- What's that?
- *Duncan:* Just doing things. Last Saturday someone started throwing bottles and we all got in.
- What happened?
- *Duncan:* Nothing really.

And:

- What do you do?
- *Albert:* Sometimes we get into mischief.
- Mischief?
- *Albert:* Well somebody gets a weird idea into their head, and they start to carry it out, and others join in.
- Weird ideas?
- *Albert:* Things . . like going around smashing milk bottles.

Classifications in their Social Context, eds. R. Ellen and D. A. Reason, Academic Press 1979, p. 230.
[27] Paul Corrigan, 'Doing Nothing', *Working Papers in Cultural Studies,* Nos. 7/8 (1975), pp.103-5.

Corrigan comments:

It is the 'weird idea' that represents the major something in 'doing nothing'. In fighting boredom the kids do not choose the street as a wonderfully lively place, rather they look upon it as the place where there is the most chance that something will happen. Doing nothing on the street must be compared with the alternatives: for example, knowing that nothing will happen with Mum and Dad in the front room; being almost certain that the youth club will be full of boredom. This makes the street the place where something might just happen, if not this Saturday, then surely next.

This is apposite, though one might want to explore further that tricky notion of 'boredom' and the differences between (sub-)cultural groupings in their labelling, and experiencing, of particular ways of 'doing nothing' as 'boring' (for example, sunbathing).

One might also draw a certain comparison between waiting 'where something might just happen' and the 'waiting', or aimless prowling, that often characterizes a scientific researcher or 'creative' writer who also hopes that a 'weird idea', outside the given and expected matrix, will 'happen'. Such a comparison might include a consideration of 'deadlines' as a particular (often occupationally related) way of structuring time, a mode of time-horizon different from both the endlessly deferrable 'if not this Saturday, then surely the next' and the relatively reliable 'something to look forward to the next day'.

In interviews with wives of soldiers embarked upon the Falklands expedition in 1982 a certain shift of horizon mode could be traced between the initial 'waiting' period as the battle fleet sailed towards the Falklands and the quite different 'expectancy' once actual combat had begun. From that example a more general exploration might reach out to include shifts in time-sense implicated in a latent or actualized awareness of the possibility of nuclear war—a matter in which deep generational differences might also be significant.

In his 'The Cultural Meaning of Drug Abuse',[28] Paul Willis quotes one 'acid'-taker:

> *Robin:* 'Dope' has a certain amount of freedom, as a result of, of . . being much more aware of what is, you know, . . what is rather than what was or will be. You know . . er'm . . I believe that one must live in the present, you know, this instant, now, experiencing now for what it is, because it is, because it is for no other reason. I suppose I could have gone into a monastery and meditated and, perhaps, found out the same thing in about fifty years, I've just found out how to do it, acid just speeded up the process of it, you know, well quite considerably.

Willis himself comments:

> This encapsulation by the 'now', and the feeling of freedom to 'walk around and feel the moment', led to a total breakdown of conventional notions of time. Industrial and job-oriented time is crucially concerned with order, i.e., what needs to be done before something else can be done—a massive critical path of consciousness . . External coercion of time experience in this way is not always humanely relevant, as we can see from the very common feelings of boredom and frustration on the shopfloor . . The heads felt the inappropriate-ness of conventional time particularly powerfully in the course of a 'trip'.

Willis then quotes another 'acid'-taker:

> *Norman:* You realise that time is man-made, there is no such thing as 'time', it's a load of cock, something that man has made to computerise himself by.

There are various aspects of these extracts that would repay comment, but Norman's remark suggests three important lines of inquiry.

---

[28] Paul Willis, "The Cultural Meaning of Drug Abuse', *WPCS*, Nos 7/8, pp. 106-18.

First, is there a degree of irreducibility in 'time' such that no possible human society could ignore certain 'givens'? At various levels one could argue that the domain of 'given' organizations of time has been steadily reduced, by the encroachment into night-time with artificial lighting, the extension of life-expectancy, the relaxing of natural agricultural temporalities with fertilizers, deliberate breeding processes and biotechnology, the deliberate modification of fertility rhythms, etc.

But then, secondly, the claim that 'time is man-made' would have to be probed to disclose the specific 'men' involved in the control and encouragement of particular ways of reducing the domain of given time, and Norman's final phrase, 'something that man has made to computerise himself by', suggests one instance where that analysis is increasingly necessary.

Thirdly, it is possible that a new form of capitalist reorganization of time is under way, in the development of a range of new technologies, all of which may reshape our time-sense, whether in the rapidation of information distribution or the restructuring of work-processes, the development of video (a private re-scheduling of the 'given' *TV Times*) or the perpetuation of large-scale and long-term unemployment.

Already the tendencies being encouraged for employment to move from 'over-time' and 'shift-work' to 'flexi-time' and from 'full-time' to 'job-sharing' are indicative of changing forms of control over labour-time.[29] The emergence of 'inflation' as an important constituent of popular economic awareness opens up gaps between different, largely class-based, forms of response, in terms of financial planning and speculative opportunism. The extension of mortgaged house-ownership has probably already had an effect upon working-class conceptions of 'life-plans', perhaps in sharp conflict with the shrinking horizons registered in a consciousness of increasing job-

---

[29] See, for example. *Work and Society Newsletter*, No. 1 (1983).

obsolescence and the possibilities of periodic redundancy and retraining.

Clearly a great many facets of contemporary life under capitalism could be analysed in terms of the construction and reconstruction of time. But if one impetus in contemporary cultural studies has been a commitment to exploring residual and emergent areas of resistance or countervailing values it may become part of the agenda of cultural studies to attend to alternative conceptions of time already in process of formation.

In that difficult project an awareness of the sometimes contradictory character of previous attempts to restructure social time-sense may be of value. Two examples from different periods can indicate this.

Christopher Hill and Keith Thomas[30] have both traced the campaign by seventeenth-century English Puritans to eradicate the many feast-days of the mediaeval church, which occasioned up to a hundred non-working days each year, and instead to regularize the week as consisting of six working days and one rest day, the Sabbath. This was an important step towards the modern homogenization of time, as uniform in quality. Yet by their very emphasis upon the observance of the Sabbath the Puritans themselves tended to foster the endowment of Sunday with 'mystical' attributes, with a peculiar quality of its own. As Thomas remarks: '[not] even the Puritans were able to emancipate themselves fully from the assumption that time was uneven in quality and that some occasions were inherently more propitious for performing critical actions than others.'

---

[30] Christopher Hill, *Society and Puritanism in Pre-Revolutionary England*, Secker and Warburg, 1964, Ch. 5; Keith Thomas, *Religion and the Decline of Magic*, Penguin 1973, pp. 742-5.

The second example is from Catalonia in the 1890s.[31] The tenancies of the peasant farmers were based upon a contract measured not in years or in human lifetimes (as, e.g., in Ireland) but in terms of the life of the vines: the land reverted to the landowner when three-quarters of the planted vines had died *(rabassa morte*—the peasants were known as *rabassaires)*. Brenan writes: 'The Catalan peasants had made an art of prolonging the life of the vines and in the old days they lasted as a rule for fifty years. This assured the labourer a contract that would cover his working life and remunerate him for the six or eight years of fruitless labour that young vines require before they mature'. But in the 1890s the phylloxera plague attacked European vineyards, eradicating the old stock of vine. The landowners imported phylloxera-resistant vines from America but these 'required much more care and labour and had a maximum life of only twenty-five years', which span was now, as far as the landowners were concerned, the legal limit of the tenancies. The eventual response of the *rabassaires* was to organize themselves for the first time into an agricultural syndicate under the leadership of Luis Companys, a lawyer who was to become in 1933 the leader of the Catalan coalition of 'left' political parties — hardly an outcome the landowners would have welcomed.

6: Conclusion

This tentative mosaic of an essay could conclude with suggestions as to lines of research into the cultural construction of time, and the associated methodological difficulties—for example, the problem of how to probe the relations between personal, gendered and class-shaped images of time, or the intriguing possibility of developing an

---

[31] See Raymond Carr, *Spain 1805-1975,* Clarendon Press 1982, p. 420f.; Gerald Brenan, *The Spanish Labyrinth,* Cambridge University Press 1960, p. 277f.

'architecture' of time akin to the construction, even creation, of habitable space in physical architecture.

The relation between cultural sub-groupings, specific forms of time-awareness and particular modes of political consciousness might be explored, for example in different immigrant communities.

Different modes of personal periodization, especially in relation to acknowledged crisis moments or significant years within a general history (e.g., 1945, 1956, 1968), might repay analysis.

The continuing, even if decayed, role of 'special occasions', individual or collective, in both punctuating and revealing the character of mundane time may still illuminate the residual resistances in all our lives to dominant modes of time-organization.

Even within a capitalist framework, the question of 'how much' we really consider our time to be 'worth' can often provoke deep-felt responses which would be susceptible to investigation.

But the peculiarly 'individual' character of time—its literal non-alienability, the fact that in one sense we cannot choose *not* to 'use' our time, or that from one angle each new birth can indeed be seen as a unique 'income-addition' to social time—indicates the difficulty of elaborating any coherent method of research for a 'cultural study of time' or even a sociology of time, as section 3 has already suggested.

Perhaps, therefore, this essay can most appropriately conclude simply by offering two further quotations for consideration—quotations themselves being a form of temporal embedding.

The first is from an American social historian, the second from a German Marxist critic.

People who have not been 'famous' or who have not participated jointly in a common cause, such as a labour movement, a strike, or an organised political or social activity, experience great difficulty in making the connection between their own lives and the historical

29

process. Without such linkages, in most instances in the United States oral-history interviewing remains a private exercise . . The former Amoskeag workers frequently replied with 'Why ask me? My story is not special' or 'What is so important about my life?' . . Attitudes changed drastically, however, after the exhibition 'Amoskeag: A Sense of Place, A Way of Life' opened in Manchester in 1975 . . Thousands of people, mostly former mill workers and their families, came to see the exhibit. Former workers, now elderly, searched the huge historic group portraits for their relatives; grandparents led their grandchildren through the exhibit, often describing how they did their jobs of thirty to forty years earlier . . The sudden opportunity to view their own lives as part of a significant historical experience provided a setting for collective identification. Under these circumstances, interviewing ceased to be an isolated individual experience. It turned, instead, into a shared community event.[32]

The awareness that they are about to make the continuum of history explode is characteristic of the revolutionary classes at the moment of their action. The great revolution introduced a new calendar. The initial day of a calendar serves as a historical time-lapse camera. And, basically, it is the same day that keeps recurring in the guise of holidays, which are days of remembrance. Thus the calendars do not measure time as clocks do; they are monuments of a historical consciousness of which not the slightest trace has been apparent in Europe in the past hundred years. In the July revolution an incident occurred which showed this consciousness still alive. On the first evening of the fighting it turned out that the clocks in towers were being fired on simultaneously and independently from several places in Paris . .

[32] Tamara K. Hareven, *Family Time and Industrial Time,* Cambridge University Press, 1982, pp. 378-9.

Historicism rightly culminates in universal history. Materialistic historiography differs from it as to method more clearly than from any other kind. Its method is additive; it musters a mass of data to fill the homogeneous, empty time. Materialistic historiography on the other hand is based on a constructive principle. Thinking involves not only the flow of thoughts, but their arrest as well. Where thinking suddenly stops in a configuration pregnant with tensions, it gives that configuration a shock, by which it crystallises into a monad.

A historical materialist approaches a historical subject only where he encounters it as a monad. In this structure he recognises the sign of a Messianic cessation of happening, or, put differently, a revolutionary chance in the fight for the oppressed past.[33]

---

[33] Walter Benjamin, *Illuminations*, pp. 263-5.

A Matter of Time by J. D. Hutton

Reviewed by Antonio Ford

'Economy of time, this is wherein ultimately all economy resolves itself.' This laconic claim by Karl Marx, in the *Grundrisse*, forms the epigraph to Jenny Hutton's new work. I rather wish that she had attended to its implications in her own writing: ironically, her book is approximately two-thirds longer than it need have been — a fact, however, which she has the grace at one point to acknowledge, even to exploit.

The first part is the main culprit. In three main sections she surveys an immense field, much of which this reviewer found yawningly familiar: the development of coinage, measurement, and abstract philosophical thought in early Greek civilisation; the gradual mechanisation of the world-picture from late antiquity to the seventeenth century and the (linked) re-definition of the virtue of 'temperance'; the slow construction of a time-discipline appropriate to industrial capitalism from the late middle ages to the early twentieth century, from the invention of mechanical clocks to the imposition of the production conveyor-belt.

It is this last development which seems most germane to her theme, and her excursions into the various preconditions for our present dominant sense of time were surely unnecessary and a little self-indulgent. One can presumably recognise what is at stake in Franklin's advice to young tradesmen, that 'time is money', without relating it to Newton's cosmology or his time at the Royal Mint, still less to any putative links between Lydian merchants, pre-Socratic philosophers and Aristotle's *Physics*. Nor do we need to know, for example, that the expansion of railways in mid-nineteenth-century Britain involved the extension of 'London time' to the whole country, in order to appreciate the fact that a complex industrial and commercial economy ideally requires a uniform time-base from which to coordinate its interconnections.

Far from historically illuminating for me the 'social homogenization and thrifty intensification of time-awareness' (a characteristic phrase from p. 384), Ms. Hutton's initial 400 pages merely reinforced my phenomenological endorsement of 'capitalist time' in the form of a deeply felt and growing impatience. Any reader already familiar with the work of, say, George Thomson, Alfred Sohn-Rethel, E. J. Dijksterhuis, E. P. Thompson, David Landes and Nigel Thrift, is strongly advised to begin Ms Hutton's volume at p. 405.

Here the argument begins to bite, mildly. Her basic point is that at the core of Marx's economic analysis of capitalism is a concept, that of 'socially necessary labour-time', which is deeply 'impregnated' (her curious word) with a 'capitalist conceptualisation of time'. One might murmur that this seems precisely apposite to any accurate analysis of capitalism, but Ms. Hutton prefers to regard this particular notion as having 'latently deflected' (*sic!*) most nineteenth- and twentieth-century European attempts to 'conceptualise socialism'.

I would myself have thought that the emphasis of marxism was not to 'conceptualise' the world but actually to change it, but her formulation has some irritant value. Fortunately, she is only indirectly concerned with the entangled debate on the intellectual credibility of Marx's so-called 'labour theory of value'; her concern is rather that attempts to derive some relatively concrete model of a post-capitalist economy, including those derived from Marx's analysis of capitalism, have retained a reliance upon 'socially necessary labour-time', in some form or another, as a crucial conceptual prop.

She first of all locates this covert appeal behind not only some rightly-forgotten nineteenth-century 'Utopian' programmes for the replacement of money by 'labour-tokens' but also such familiar 'Labourist rhetorical priorities' as the 'equalisation' of wealth and income. Both of these she sees as mere variations upon an underlying triple equation of money, labour and time, all three conceived along an axis of homogeneous measurement units.

She next analyses the emergence of Soviet economic planning in the 1920s, linking it both to the Taylorisation of factory work-processes and to the extraordinary proliferation of officially encouraged 'time-budget' sociological studies in the early Soviet Union. Here again she claims that the 'key operative concept' was the 'abstractly homogeneous character of time', with time as both the immediate measure of labour-efficiency and the ultimate measure of money, itself the primary 'organisational means' of State allocation of productive resources to 'socially necessary labour'.

In this analysis, however, a certain fissure appears between 'socially necessary labour' and 'labour-time', with 'homogeneous time' as the core concept of State planning operating as an 'organisational mediation', whether directly in the form of Five-Year Plans or indirectly in the exaltation of Stakhanovite work-norms: the 'primary drive of the entire Soviet economic motor' was, she claims, 'a race against abstract time'. (I would myself have thought it mainly a race for security against far from abstract Western hostility.)

In a brief aside she indicates that this alleged fissure between socially necessary labour and labour-time took a radically different form in the Chinese Cultural Revolution, but she postpones discussion of this and returns instead to Western Europe and the present, suggesting a 'reverse parallel' (whatever contorted geometry that term might derive from) with the Soviet experience. In the wake of massive and long-term structural unemployment (those easy phrases . .) she maintains that most 'socialists' (her scare quotes) have proposed merely short-term demands focused upon a reduction in 'average labour-time' as a means to a 'redistribution of socially-available necessary labour' (i.e. crudely but less conceptually put: job-sharing) while retaining an equation between labour-time and money (i.e. minimal loss of average pay) as an organisational means of somewhat covertly redistributing income.

All this, however, she castigates as merely 'capitalist labour-time allocation stood on its head' (another appealingly clumsy phrasing!) and in any case as in itself both politically unlikely and economically unviable, since such a demand implies both the pre-condition of adequate coercive power over international capitalist enterprises and a continued endemic misfit between total purchasing power and total earned income (i.e., in her view, an inflation-deflation cycle).

The logical resolution of this 'incoherence', according to Ms. Hutton, would be State control of capitalist enterprise and a fully 'planned' economy—but that is precisely the recipe which informed both early Soviet and traditional Labour-socialist thinking, i.e. for Ms. Hutton most 'left' responses to the current crisis of employment embed yet more permutations upon an underlying economic model fundamentally shaped by the insidious notion of 'socially necessary labour-time'.

By this point in her lengthy but not very lucid discussion I was both irritated and intrigued. Ms Hutton seemed to have argued herself into an impossible corner. If her overall argument was correct then only an abandonment of the very notion of 'socially necessary labour-time' in any form whatsoever could satisfy her idea of socialism, yet any 'conceptualisation' of an economic system would seem to require some notion of overall social allocation of jobs and with it, therefore, of 'labour-time'. This is what intrigued me.

What irritated me was the slipperiness (to be kind) of her actual arguments. For example, I am simply not convinced that a sensible redeployment of labour, eradicating 'overtime', reducing average weekly hours, extending job-sharing schemes and the like, while maintaining a firm incomes policy and (perhaps) a national minimum wage, would necessarily involve either coercive direction of industry or an unstable national currency; such a programme seems to me eminently rational and pragmatic.

I can quite see that it would qualify neither as Ms. Hutton's 'socialism' nor as a long-term solution to structural unemployment, but that is no justification for cavalier dismissal. Nor do I admit the 'parallel' she draws between the alleged 'logic' of Labour Party socialism and the basic model of Soviet planning; the latter has more in common with the early, forced phases of capitalist industrialisation (as her own Part I, section (iii) should have reminded her), while the former is characterised by a humane flexibility rather than by any rigid 'logic'.

However, the details of her 'arguments' are perhaps less important than the peculiarity of her own 'logic'. It would seem that *any* implicit reliance upon a conception of time as homogeneous—in other words as composed of abstractly equatable units—is enough to characterise an economic system for Ms Hutton as 'impregnated' with capitalism—presumably implying that capitalism would re-emerge from the womb of any such system.

Yet on her own evidence — a full 400 pages of it — that very notion of time not only pre-dates capitalism but also deeply permeates the whole fabric of Western thought. Which is why, despite my impatience and irritation, I remained intrigued enough to persevere with the next section of this sprawling volume.

*

It begins abruptly, even impolitely, with a peculiarly silly question: 'How long has it taken you to read this far?' It proceeds to even sillier questions, such as 'How long did it take you to understand the argument on page 174?' I confess that I found it difficult even to locate an argument on page 174—to which, no doubt, Ms Hutton would respond by asking me how long I looked for one or how long it took me not to find one!

The point of these questions is presumably the simple-minded one that each reader will have a different answer, or even that an 'answer' is impossible to give (does one include coffee-breaks, answering the phone, checking a reference, going off to read a cited article previously unknown to one — or just calculate the physical turning of the pages?). Yet I reject the further implication that the obvious incommensurability of different readers' rates of reading and

36

comprehension somehow undermines the notion that time is homogeneous, since whatever answer one gave would still have to be couched in terms of some public unit of measurement. I admit, warily, that an appropriate (if, in this case, horrifying) answer might be 'a lifetime', but even a lifetime is measurable in years — insurance companies do it all the time. But if Ms. Hutton thinks these peculiar questions are relevant to the problem of organising an economic system I remain wholly sceptical.

Nor does her next series of questions at all persuade me. She asks, for example, 'How long did it take you to mend the fence/ clear out the attic/ wallpaper the bedroom? ' Again, these seem to me stupendously inept questions in this context, not only because in my own case such factors as personal skill, degrees of motivation and temperamental procrastination are involved, but because one could reasonably assimilate such tasks to a wage-rate based upon how long the job ought to take a competent professional. If Ms. Hutton intends to suggest some qualitative difference (apart from sheer frustration) between my use of my 'own' time on such chores and the time taken by a decently employed gardener or decorator, then she is merely reminding us that in some cultures 'time' is indeed conceived of as task-time rather than wage-time.

I admit some puzzlement or doubt as to the very validity of her next series of questions, which are variations upon: 'How long did it take for you to have your last idea?' The precise formulation is odd here: not 'how long did it take you' but 'for you' — implying perhaps that some at least of that immeasurable time (a point I partly concede) was not only 'my' time, since arguably some ideas are historically unthinkable before the development of other ideas: one couldn't have an 'idea' in nuclear physics before the discovery of the atom.

Again, however, the wider claim Ms. Hutton seems to be suggesting is surely misguided: we can and do assign a certain measurable temporality even to the process of thinking, by, for example, commissioning research within a firm deadline and expecting it to be met (President

Kennedy's promise to land a man on the moon in ten years), and we can often, in our own case at least, estimate fairly precisely how long a certain intellectual task will take (writing this review for instance). Moreover, we have conventional ways of paying for intellectual work, even—or particularly—when it has involved a long period of gestation or prior dedication, training and practice, as in the case of painters, lawyers, professors, or even reviewers.

Admittedly, our sense of the exact 'value' of such work is dictated not by 'how long' it took but by its artistic quality, its competence, its intellectual worth, etc. It seems that Ms. Hutton would assimilate all of these distinct criteria of quality to the marxist notion of 'use-value', since her next step is to return to Marx. Much of this is familiar enough. She makes the usual points, that for Marx capitalism is geared to the production of exchange-values rather than use-values, that labour-power is unequally exchanged as the commodity which produces commodities, and that the main 'contradiction' developing within capitalism is that between the material forces of production and the social relations of production. She does a rather tedious job of explaining her own understanding of these notoriously opaque terms, devoting a surprising number of pages to elucidation of a theory which she seemed earlier to regard as crucially flawed for her main purpose.

Some aspects of her account were, however, unfamiliar and one or two controversial. I was, for example, struck by her use of a passage from *The German Ideology*:

> . . with a communist organisation of society, there disappears the subordination of the artist to local and national narrowness, which arises entirely from division of labour, and also the subordination of the artist to some definite art, thanks to which he is exclusively a painter, sculptor, etc., the very name of his activity adequately expressing the narrowness of his professional development and his dependence on division of labour. In a communist society there are no painters but at most people who engage in painting among other activities.

Rather amusingly, she amends this passage to apply variously to plumbers, physicists and pole-vaulters, her case being that for Marx a communist society is not organised on the basis of job-allocation—or even diverse 'part-time' activities—but that the very concept of 'a definitely-named job-definition' (her usual verbal goulash) has been 'surpassed'. (Quite what this would mean for those of us who prefer the intense Englishness of a Constable to the rootless talent of a Picasso she doesn't say. Nor could she find a place for my local plumber who alone understands the intricacies of my Edwardian hot-water system, but let that pass.)

More surprising than this predictable Utopian woolliness is an unusually sustained argument in which she seeks to show that in Marx's theory the real motor of history is — of all things — 'ideas'! Her reading of Marx puts a quite rigorous emphasis upon the 'primacy of the material forces of production' in any development of the 'preconditions of social change' but, as she puts it with rare colloquial vigour, 'material forces of production are of no earthly use if no-one has any idea what to do with them.'

This logically leads her to the claim that it is *'new ideas'* about what to use in production and how to use it that underpin any major development of production, though she also recognises that the emergence of such 'new ideas' is often closely connected with actual production and is inevitably shaped by human desires, needs and curiosity, all 'profoundly produced from within an existing social matrix yet also premised upon a proleptic idea of possibilities not currently contained within that matrix' (I much prefer her colloquial prose).

What more orthodox marxist materialists or determinists will make of this argument I don't know — but she makes effective use of Marx's own writings as an example of a 'new idea crystallised within yet pointing beyond the parameters of a particular socio-intellectual paradigm' (*ugh*). Presumably for her the notion of 'socially necessary labour-time' is precisely an index to Marx's own 'intrication'(!) within the 'matrix' he 'proleptically surpassed'.

After 550 pages of this coagulated prose, it was at least a relief to reach the final section of the book.

It opens promisingly, with a joke: that magnificently unequal exchange between Eccles and Bluebottle in *A Punch Up the Conker*, which begins:

Bluebottle: What time is it, Eccles?

Eccles: Just a minute. I've got it writted down here on a piece of paper. A nice man wrote the time down for me this morning.

Bluebottle: Oh. Then why do you carry it around with you, Eccles ?

Eccles: Well. If any body asks me the time I can show it to them.

Bluebottle: Wait a minute, Eccles, my good man.

Eccles: What is it, fellow?

Bluebottle: It's writted on this bit of paper, what it is 8 o'clock, is writted.

Eccles: I know that, my good fellow. That's right. When I asked the fellow to write it down it was 8 o'clock.

Bluebottle: Well then, supposing when somebody asks you the time it isn't 8 o'clock?

Eccles: Then I don't show it to them.

Bluebottle: Oh. Well, how do you know when it's 8 o'clock ?

Eccles: I've got it written down on a piece of paper.

Bluebottle: I wish I could afford a piece of paper with the time written on. Here, Eccles, let me hold that piece of paper to my ear would you . . Here, this piece of paper ain't going.

Eccles: What! I've been sold a forgery!

Bluebottle: No wonder it stopped at 8 o'clock.

Eccles: Oh dear.

Bluebottle: You should get one of them things my grandad's got. His firm gave it to him when he retired. It's one of them things what it is that wakes you up at 8 o'clock, boils the kettule and pours a cup of tea.

Eccles: Oh yea — what's it called ... erm ... ?

Bluebottle: My grandma.

Eccles: Wait a minute. How does she know when it's 8 o'clock?

Bluebottle: She's got it written down on a piece of paper.

—and so on. (Sadly, Mr Milligna's copyright fees deter this reviewer from quoting more.)

Ms Hutton poses two linked questions about this exchange: how are jokes produced and how are they distributed? I confess, as indeed she does, to a certain bafflement as to how jokes are 'originally' produced (and perhaps neither Freud nor Spike Milligan could help us very much), but I accept her fairly harmless claim that the 'distribution' of jokes normally involves a kind of reproduction rather than simple repetition and that this reproduction usually employs only the resources of our own physical bodies. The implications of this banality fascinate Ms Hutton sufficiently for her to spend several pages elaborating it, but the point is reasonably obvious.

She next extends the same basic analysis to songs, and again I have no major quarrel with her. But she then advances to the 're-production' of what she calls 'art-ideas'. I would be tempted to characterise this passage as an unabashed avowal of artistic plagiarism. She recounts how, as a student, she used to prowl art galleries and exhibitions looking for aesthetically pleasing modem sculptures and paintings which she was able to 'make for herself out of scrap materials at home'. I doubt if her miniature Anthony Caros or recreated Mondriaans gave much aesthetic pleasure or edification to anyone else, but in principle her claim seems valid (it is one of my objections to much modern art): that the basic or even detailed 'idea', scheme, or formal pattern of a particular work of art could be deliberately reconstructed from easily available materials, with relatively little practical 'skill' involved. That the plagiarist (or forger) could introduce individual variations seems to her simply on a par with a personal rendition of a folk-song or phrasing of a joke.

Her next target (or victim) for appropriative imitation seems to have been modern furniture, and even interior design, in equipping her student bed-sit. No doubt such practices are more common than the proprietors of Habitat would care to think and are, I suppose, encouraged by an early addiction to knitting or dress-making from Vogue patterns. Ms. Hutton traces her ethically dubious career along these lines to encompass a rather surprising, even impressive, range of other people's designs and commodities.

Her serious intent, over and above mere autobiographical self-congratulation, begins to emerge as she successively lists, with each new 'acquisition', the tools she also purchased, borrowed or — it seems — made for herself (on the basis no doubt of thoughtful visits to her local tool-merchant or her crafty scanning of manufacturers' catalogues!). From this point, however, it is difficult to tell how far she departs from veracious anecdote and ventures into fantasy. Faced with a tricky spot of welding, she perhaps did have recourse to equipment in her local school's handicrafts workshop (as it happens, domestic oxyacetylene welders can be easily hired anyway, at least in the States), but I am disinclined to believe that she could ever have 'borrowed' the facilities of a Government Retraining Centre to make a new door for her car, or that she made herself a working telephone (outgoing calls only, but uncharged) 'with the help of a friend'. Certainly by this time she must have exhausted, even exceeded, the range of do-it-yourself projects catalogued in the *Readers' Digest Home Maintenance Manual*, ambitiously comprehensive as that is.

It should now be apparent what her basic point is: that in most of our purchases of durable commodities we certainly pay for materials and for someone else's labour-time but we also pay for the knowledge and skill (the 'idea' of the object, in her terms) and for the machines and tools used. Yet we can relatively easily appropriate much of the design-knowledge and even requisite skill and we can often gain access to the necessary tools and machines.

Two detailed proposals emerge here, which for Ms. Hutton are apparently steps on the way to her socialism: that there should be publicly owned 'work-shops' equipped with a wide range of tools and machines, and secondly that the requisite 'production knowledge' should be widely and freely available.

She concentrates first on the latter aspect. There are three main ways, she argues, in which this aim can be achieved. First, by an emphasis upon production knowledge in schools, aimed not at 'training for jobs' but, in the first instance, at domestic do-it-yourself competence, confidence, and even self-sufficiency. This she envisages in a concrete form, of a school undertaking, for example, to build, equip and maintain actual houses for old age pensioners.

Second, she wants a 're-design programme' giving priority to the re-design of all common articles of use so that they can be not only maintained but actually made with relatively little technical expertise and with tools and machines that can be made easily available for public use. Again, the educational sector is to play a role, with redesign commissions along these lines to technical colleges, art schools and universities.

Third, she proposes an 'access programme', in which all production knowledge is made publicly and freely available, both in the form of computer data-banks and through a register of available 'teaching' personnel, both of these coordinated through the network of public work-shops. These latter she envisages, it seems, as a cross between a small-batch production factory and an adult education technical centre, but based on the principle that anyone can use their facilities to make rather than buy what they want. The problem of 'payment' for materials and facilities she postpones.

In themselves, these are not particularly 'Utopian' proposals. They indeed extrapolate from some familiar features or growing tendencies in our present 'socio-intellectual matrix'. Secondary education has long imposed a certain amount of 'workshop' knowledge, not to speak of traditional 'domestic science' upon reluctant pupils. The DIY industry is already significant, involving a considerable degree of incipient 're-design' (quite startlingly in such areas as plumbing), while the general de-skilling of many production-line jobs in the wake of the microelectronics revolution does, I suppose, have the kind of reverse-side potential upon which Ms Hutton clearly relies.

The increasingly sophisticated development of multi-function robotics, numerically-controlled machine-tools, computer-aided design, modular instrumentation and terotechnology, leading to radically reduced maintenance requirements in factories, does perhaps make the provision of small-scale and very versatile 'workshops' feasible. The even more rapid advances in information technology certainly indicate the technical possibility of a vast extension of instantly-available production-patterns, instruction-sets, and even feedback-controlled computer-assisted production machines reprogrammable for a wide range of products, upon which any computer-literate person (or even, given effective graphics, VDU-reader) could successfully perform a reasonably complicated production-process.

Nevertheless, the convergent implications of Ms. Hutton's proposals are, I think, very radical indeed. The very term she favours, 'work-shops', indicates a fusion of activities with rather drastic implications for the local High Street or shopping precinct, not only for proprietors but for distributors, packaging companies, accountants, advertisers and sales-assistants. By, in effect, cutting out all 'middle-men' between 'producer' and 'consumer' (so far, though, only in consumer durables?) a very extensive re-distribution of social labour is implied, and with it a far-reaching re-organisation of individual and social 'time'.

For example, a great deal of time is currently absorbed in the transportation of finished products, in stock-taking, display, etc., and in 'shopping around' for the 'right' product. If one were able simply to enter a workshop and 'reproduce' what one wanted from an available pattern or electronic template (much as one can now mix one's own choice of decorating paints in some shops), the effect could be as devastating as the impact of cassette-recorders on the record industry or of videotapes on cinema attendance. Yet the total 'time' involved for the individual re-producer in, say, fully equipping a house, might not be very great — and it would be time directly involved in production for use not for exchange. Presumably, too, it would be open to any individual to feed any bright new ideas for making products into the general data-bank.

Ms. Hutton is clearly attracted by these last points, and they apparently override for her the loss (not least in social time) of economies of scale in such a dispersed organisation of production.

A number of other obvious problems she does, however, consider. The first is the provision of such workshops and the control of them. Here it seems that her proposals are deliberately 'transitional', envisaged as able to be developed from the already-present possibilities towards an ultimately very different future. It is also clear that her 'present' is, quite decisively, the most advanced form of technological industrial capitalism: one could hardly implement her 'idea' in much of the Third World.

Thus, she has no hesitation in seeing the building and equipping of such workshops as the initial responsibility of national and local government, arguing that the present level of government financing of capitalist commercial industry, in grants, taxation provision and direct investment (amounting in the UK to over 50 per cent of industrial capital investment) makes a gradually extending programme of such work-shops perfectly feasible.

She applies the same argument to a redirection of present government-sponsored research and development towards commissioned re-design projects leading to government-held patents. But she also envisages the building and equipping of such centres themselves as eventually shaped by the same production-for-use principle: that the resources of one centre would enable another to be built by those demanding one in their more immediate locality (presumably when the queues for use of the resources become as long as the present dole queues!).

Forms of 'payment' for use of workshop facilities cause her little hesitation. She is naively optimistic about the development of 'alternative' renewable energy sources for such workshops, listing a locally variable repertoire or 'cocktail' of solar, wind, wave, hot-rock and biomass forces as making possible a major reliance upon workshop-generated power and thus reducing energy 'costs' to a minimum. Second, she wants an extension of the 'grant support' principle to cover the remaining energy and maintenance costs of such centres on a par with hospitals, schools, municipal sports facilities, etc.

For the 'cost' of materials (including the transportation costs of basic 'raw' materials for each centre) she finds herself reaching for what is surely her own variation upon a scheme based on 'socially necessary labour-time'. She proposes, in effect, a redirection of labour into the production of 'primary materials', with work in a 'primary industry' (the level at which the workshops themselves are 'supplied') as one component of a 're-division of labour-lifetime' (a patently fudging phrase!). She apparently sees us all as 'qualifying' for use of workshop materials by virtue of some contribution to 'primary' production at some (limited) period of our lives, rather as one might now be 'entitled' to three years of higher education at some self-chosen moment in a life. The traditional, and surely bankrupt, character of this 'idea' is partly obfuscated by her elaboration of a number of allied notions.

The central claim here is that an economy reduced to paid (and taxed?) labour only in 'primary' production, with a great many secondary and finished-product sectors effectively eradicated, would be amenable to 'price calculation' upon a Sraffian model, i.e. by a system of social accounting derived directly from the concrete physical data of production, as in Piero Sraffa's *The Production of Commodities by Commodities*. In a sense, she argues that while Marx's correct analysis of capitalism has proved inappropriate for conceptualising socialism, Sraffa's inadequate model of capitalism can be developed to provide a basic model of a socialist economy.

To achieve this bizarre reading of Sraffa's (deceptively simple) argument she particularly insists upon four aspects of his analysis. First, that the terms 'profit' and 'wages' in Sraffa's terminology can be systematically replaced by 'social appropriation' ('taxes'?) and by 'personal income', without modifying the logic of his case. Second, that her notion of 'primary' production can be successfully approximated to Sraffa's term 'basic commodity'. Third, that Sraffa's theoretical proof that in any actual economic system there is embedded a miniature standard system which can be brought to light by chipping off the unwanted parts (para. 26) offers a real practical basis for price calculation within a 'reduced' economic system of the kind she sketches. And lastly, that Sraffa's insistence that the rate of profits, as a ratio, has a significance which is independent of any prices, and can well be 'given' before the prices are fixed,; it is accordingly susceptible of being determined from outside the system of production, in particular by the level of the money rates of interest (para. 44). All of which suggests the feasibility, within her system, of determining the overall proportion or ratio of 'social appropriation' to 'personal income', and the level of 'wages' and 'prices' (exchange ratios), by deliberately political decisions, guided by physical data calculations — i.e. the required capacity of the 'primary' production sectors.

As a non-economist, all I can do is relay Ms Hutton's basic points, as I partially understand them, and I humbly recommend that you read Piero Sraffa for yourself, bearing them critically in mind. But I at least remain unconvinced, certainly by her third and fourth points. I am also wholly sceptical concerning her 'practical' application of this theoretical position.

She elaborates a notion of 'regional standard systems' or sub-systems (the terms are derived from Sraffa), based, it would seem, not upon geographical regions but upon composite 'units' or wards of democratic control defined according to approximate self-sufficiency in crucial areas of primary production. This seems to imply that one might live in Manchester but be a 'citizen' of the same political 'unit' or constituency as an area of Wales (providing water reservoirs), a percentage of Sheffield steel-mills, and a number of East Anglian farms! Not even Athenian democracy, in all its complexities of citizen identification and multiple definiton of *demes*, ever tried to operate quite such an outrageously unwieldy structure!

It should be clear that Ms Hutton's harmless *Goon Show* joke has finally led her to the usual Utopian absurdities, and it seems pointless to pursue her wilder fancies into the realms of, for example, agriculture and international finance, or to recapitulate her familiar programmes for workers' control of primary production. To her credit she disarmingly remarks that detailed Utopias only seem impossibly complex to those who have never seriously attempted a systematic description of how our present economic, political and social system actually manages to continue functioning even for a short period of time.

Ms. Hutton also recognises that her own portrait of the future is partial, incomplete and provisional, neither a manifesto nor a programme but a 'perspective'. Some conclusions may however be drawn from this ambitious, if largely futile, book.

The first is that the demise of socialist 'Utopian' thinking and imagination has perhaps been unfortunate, even for non-socialists, if only because any single attempt without a tradition to support it must seem mere wishful thinking. Perhaps a deluge of personal and idiosyncratic Utopias is now a prerequisite for any coherent sense of a feasible alternative future. (There were some two hundred 'Utopias' published in the last decades of the nineteenth century, providing a context for such brave attempts as William Morris's). The elaboration of multiple contending Utopias, extrapolating from different major emphases within the socialist tradition (as many SF dystopias have extrapolated facets of capitalism), may be necessary before a sensible sifting of the feasible and attractive from the idiotic and repugnant can occur.

Ms Hutton's emphases seem to me at least potentially interesting as political and economic starting-points: a serious re-consideration of 'production for use', an underlining of the need to socialise 'production knowledge', a deliberate programme of technical re-design rather than mere extrapolation from the existing horizon and priorities of technology, and perhaps her attempt at an appropriation of Sraffa.

I am less persuaded by her theoretical starting-point. Her apparent repudiation of 'homogeneous time' seems to me (insofar as I find it intelligible at all) largely a disguised aversion to *any* economic thinking which deploys an abstraction from 'concrete' labour to yield a viable account of how ultimately we measure 'exchange-values'. The logic of her position is indeed that she thinks primarily, and even parochially, in terms of individual or domestic 'use', whereas the traditional emphasis upon 'socially necessary labour-time' is also a way of confronting that level of social needs which are definable in practice only through the political processes which she largely displaces from the centre of her analysis. The articulation of or interaction between those perspectives is formidably difficult to formulate, but Ms Hutton seems only to have considered one, lop-sided, element within that complex dialectical process of transformation so ably summarised, for example, by Mr. Peregrine Anderson:

> Crises within modes of production are not identical with confrontations between classes. The two may or may not fuse, according to the historical situation. The onset of major economic crises, whether under feudalism or capitalism, has typically taken all social classes unawares, deriving from structural depths below those of direct conflict between them. The resolution of such crises, on the other hand, has no less typically been the outcome of prolonged war between classes.

Oddly enough, Ms Hutton somewhat redresses the balance in the body of her book by returning in an Epilogue to her postponed discussion of the Chinese Cultural Revolution, where she seeks to show that some of the basic principles she has advocated were actually implemented, however unevenly, briefly, and brutally, in a society with a radically different level of technological development. In particular, she emphasises the role of 'do-it-yourself' technical innovation and the appropriation of production 'ideas'. Personally, I do not expect, or hope, to see the transplantation of such a cultural revolution into England.

It is far more likely, in my view, that an enterprising capitalist will soon open a 'workshop' very much along Ms Hutton's lines — but on a commercially profitable basis and as an extension rather than subversion of existing capitalist priorities. And I suspect that any 'users' would be very heavily charged indeed for real access to any effective 'production knowledge'. Trade secrets are even more tightly protected than State secrets. If such a capitalist workshop were to develop it's possible, I suppose, that the entrepreneur involved would actually be fostering socialism 'unawares'. But I rather doubt it.

Antonio Ford

QUOTING TIME:
notes on Derrida's 'Ousia et Grammè' [1]

An enormous task is proposed here. The texts pointed
out are doubtless among the most difficult and most
decisive of the history of philosophy. (38)

Derrida's 'Ousia et Grammè' is a note on a footnote in *Being
and Time*, itself a note on Hegel's *Jena Logic* and *Encyclopaedia*,
on Aristotle's *Physics*, on Bergson.[2] Thus, for example,
Derrida on (Heidegger on) Hegel (on) Aristotle:

Here [in Hegel] the Aristotelian aporia is understood,
thought, and assimilated into that which is properly
dialectical. It suffices — and it is necessary — to take
things in the other sense and from the other side to
conclude that the Hegelian dialectic is but the repetition,
the paraphrastic re-edition of an exoteric paradox, the
brilliant formulation of a vulgar paradox. (43)

Yet   a   footnote   checks   this   formulation,   corrects
'paraphrastic' —

Hegel conceived his relation to the Aristotelian exoteric
. . in an entirely other category than that of the
"paraphrase" of which Heidegger speaks.
(43, note 16)

And a laconic parenthesis within the footnote further
queries the term itself:

(What is to paraphrase in philosophy?)

[1] Unless otherwise specified, page-references throughout are to Derrida,
Margins of Philosophy, trans. Alan Bass, Harvester, Brighton, 1982. Page
references preceded by *M* refer to *Marges de la philosophie*, Les Editions du
Minuit, Paris, 1972.
[2] Martin Heidegger, *Being and Time*, trans. J. Macquarrie and E. Robinson,
Blackwell, Oxford, 1967, p. 500, note xxx, referring to p. 484.
* Published in *Theory After Derrida*, ed. K. C. Baral & R. Radhakrishnan,
Routledge, New Delhi and London, 2009.

(In literary criticism it used to be a heresy.) Yet, what is the alternative? To quote, *verbatim*? (Perhaps to quote a whole previous text, since selective, partial quotation approaches paraphrase? Thus, the mediaeval Commentary. But is Derrida's 'Note' a commentary?).

At the pivotal point of his essay ('The Pivot of Essence') Derrida quotes Aristotle, *Physics* 218a 10–15, thus:

> Si en effet le maintenant est toujours autre, comme aucune partie n'est, dans le temps, en même temps (*ama*) qu'une autre . . comme le maintenant non-êtant, étant toutefois auparavant, a nécessairement été détruit à un moment donné, les maintenants ne sont pas en même temps (*ama*) les uns avec les autres, et ce qui fut auparavant a nécessairement été détruit. (*M* 61)

The reading eye hesitates, returns; recalls; repeats:

> If in fact the now is always other, and if none of the parts in time which are other are simultaneous (*hama*) . . and if the 'now' which is not, but formerly was, must have ceased to be or been destroyed at a certain moment, the 'nows' too cannot be simultaneous (*hama*) with one another, but the preceding 'now' must always have been destroyed.
> (53–54)

Remembering Aristotle's Greek, referring to other translations, we may restore, reinstate the phrase removed in Derrida's rendition:

> For if the now is always different, and if no two sectional parts of time can exist at once (*unless one includes the other, the longer the shorter*), and if the now that is not . . . (etc.)

Is the (quasi-)parenthesis merely expendable, to be repressed without loss in a paraphrastic quotation? Yet the passage from which these few lines come is, for Derrida, the pivot (*cheville*: ankle-bone) of the whole of Western metaphysics:

> Having recalled why it may be thought that time is not a being, Aristotle leaves the question in suspense . . As has been noted, there is here "a metaphysical problem that Aristotle in part, perhaps, has evaded," even if "nevertheless, he has clearly posed it." That the evaded question is properly metaphysical might be understood otherwise. What is metaphysical is perhaps less the evaded question than the *evaded* question. Metaphysics, then, may be posited by this omission. In repeating the question of Being in the transcendental horizon of time, *Being and Time* thus brings to light the omission which permitted metaphysics to believe that it could think time on the basis of a being already silently predetermined in its relation to time. (47)

That 'silent predetermination' arises most patently, for Derrida, in Aristotle's use of *hama*, which the French translates (here) as 'en même temps'. We shall return to this pivotal point. Meanwhile, Derrida continues:

> If all metaphysics is engaged by this gesture, *Being and Time*, in this regard at least, constitutes a decisive step beyond or within metaphysics . . It is what the question evades that Heidegger puts back into play from the first part of *Being and Time* on: time, then, will be that on the basis of which the Being of beings is indicated, and not that whose possibility will be derived on the basis of a being already constituted (and in secret temporally predetermined), as a present being . . (47)

The claim that Aristotle's treatment of time in *Physics* IV has a crucial status is insistently reiterated in various reformulations: '. . what is evaded in the question propagates its effects over the entire history of metaphysics, or rather constitutes this history as such, as the effect of this evasion' (47). Even more specifically, insistently:

> The entire weight of Aristotle's text comes down upon a word so small (*hama*) as to be hardly visible, and hardly visible because it appears self-evident, as discreet as that which goes without saying, a word that is self-effacing, operating all the more effectively in that it evades thematic attention. That which goes without saying, making discourse play itself out in its articulation, that which henceforth will constitute the pivot [*cheville*] (*clavis*) of metaphysics, the small key that both opens and closes the history of metaphysics in terms of what it puts at stake, the clavicle on which the conceptual decision of Aristotle bears down and is articulated, is the small word *hama*. It appears five times in 218a. (56)

But if the whole edifice of Aristotelian metaphysics, and with it the entire history of Western metaphysics, embracing even Hegel, Kant and Heidegger himself, rests upon this wobbling pivot, upon this tiny repeated word in this 'untechnical' (exoteric, cf. 217b 30) passage in this Fourth Book of one Treatise — if the vast architecture of the house of being can be tracked or traced back to this one omission or evasion — surely Derrida might at least have spared the time to quote the whole crucial paragraph without elision, without omission?

Is Derrida's replacement of Aristotle's quasi-aside (a mere qualifying exception, after all) by ellipsis a matter of evasion or merely an occasion for relentlessly pedantic quibble? Can we afford simply to forget any part of this apparently foundational aporia? Undecidedly, let us postpone the question — and first ask another.

*

"I have forgotten my umbrella."

Derrida quoting Nietzsche, *Éperons* p. 123

As Derrida himself has reminded us, we seem to need to know (or decide) what kind of (a) writing a quotation comes from in order to make sense of the quotation. What kind of (a) writing, then, is 'Ousia et Grammè'? Precisely, what 'enormous task' is proposed, or even attempted here? Perhaps it is an historical inquiry, leading to and substantiating not only the judgements on the entire history of metaphysics already quoted but also other, pithier claims: 'From Parmenides to Husserl, the privilege of the present has never been put into question' (34) and 'There is no chance that within the thematic of metaphysics anything might have budged, as concerns the concept of time, from Aristotle to Hegel' (39). Yet Derrida rejects, repudiates, a familiar kind of historical inquiry: 'without a rigorous critical and deconstructive acknowledgement of the system [of connected metaphysical concepts], the very necessary attention to differences, disruptions, mutations, leaps, restructurations, etc., becomes ensnarled in slogans, in dogmatic stupidity, in empiricist precipitation — or all of these at once' (39). Rather, 'we must . . think our relation to (the entire past of) the history of philosophy otherwise than in the style of dialectical negativity, which — as a tributary of the vulgar concept of time — posits an other present as the negation of the present past-retained-uplifted in the *Aufhebung*, where it yields its truth. It is precisely a question of something entirely other: it is the tie between truth and presence that must be thought, in a thought that henceforth may no longer need to be either true or present, and for which the meaning and value of truth are put in question in a way impossible for any intraphilosophical moment, especially for skepticism and everything that is systematic with it' (38). This rethinking of our relation to the history of philosophy in relation to, as derived from, germinating from, the concept of time, could — to begin with — revolve around that very concept of history as falling into time upon which Heidegger (it would appear) 'agrees' with Hegel:

> Time is usually considered as that in which beings are produced. Within-time-ness, intratemporality, is taken to be the homogenous medium in which the movement of daily existence is reckoned and organised. This homogeneity of the temporal medium becomes the effect of a 'levelling off of primordial time' . . and constitutes a world time more objective than the object and more subjective than the subject. In affirming that history — that is, spirit, which alone has a history — falls into time, is not Hegel thinking in terms of the vulgar concept of time? Heidegger claims to be in agreement with Hegel on this proposition in its 'results' (im Resultat) . . but . . Hegel himself has taught us that results are nothing without their becoming, outside the locus which assigns to them an itinerary or a method. (35)

Yet if from Parmenides to Husserl, from Aristotle to Hegel, the history of philosophy constitutes a 'system', a thematic within which the concept of time has not budged, the privilege of the present has never been put in question, the tie between truth and presence has been un-re-thinkable, then are not intra-philosophical moments strangely akin to intra-temporal moments (in a vulgar concept of time, of course), Western metaphysics merely a homogenous medium, in which any relation between result and becoming is, already, systemically pre-determined, any discrepancy or disruption, between premise, process and conclusion already pre-cluded?

Yet would not any such reading of the history of philosophy risk the kind of strictures once, at another time, passed upon the propositions and ambitions of structuralism: 'It is also readily demonstrable that what is in question is the metaphysics implicit in all structuralism, or in every structuralist proposition. In particular, a structuralist reading, by its own activity, always presupposes and appeals to the theological simultaneity of the book . . [Rousset:] " . . reading, which is developed in duration, will have to make the work simultaneously present in all its parts . . The only complete reading is the one which transforms the book into a simultaneous network of reciprocal relationships." . . . [Bergson:] "Duration thus takes on the illusory form of a homogenous milieu, and the union between these two terms, space and duration, is simultaneity." In this demand for the flat and the horizontal, what is intolerable for structuralism is indeed the richness implied by the volume, every element of signification that cannot be spread out into the simultaneity of a form.' (*Writing and Difference*, 24–25)

If, once again, the entire weight of Aristotle's text on time comes down upon, is deconstructed from, one tiny 'element of signification', a word so small, *hama* ('simultaneous'), as to be hardly visible, operating all the more effectively in that it evades thematic attention, can we be so sure that another, equally rigorous, nonthematic, attention to the texts on time of, say, Aquinas or Leibniz, Plotinus or Duns Scotus, would not reveal or unravel in each case quite another, non-Aristotelian conceptualisation of time, even of presence?

A parenthesis in the final footnote of Derrida's own text momentarily troubles his own overall claim concerning the history of philosophy:

> Thus Plotinus (what is his status in the history of metaphysics and in the "Platonic" era, if one follows Heidegger's reading?) who speaks of presence, that is, also of *morphē*, as the trace of nonpresence, as the amorphous. A trace which is neither absence nor presence . . (66, note 41).

Already, one might say, Plotinus in *Enneads* III, 7.7ff, had criticised and repudiated Aristotle's formulation of time as a circular definition, as already silently predetermined by a taken-for-granted notion of motion as temporal, and had offered his own counter-definition ('the life of the [universal] soul in movement as it passes from one stage of act or experience to another') which may suffer from its own circularity but leaves its considerable alternative traces in later notions of 'absolute duration' dissociated from any relation of measurability to physical motion.[3]

For example, the systematic critique of Aristotle on time by Crescas, in *Or Adonai*, Proposition XV, 2, leads to a further counter-definition ('Time is the measure of the continuity of motion or of rest between two instants') which can indeed be read as a re-wording of either Plotinus or Aristotle.[4] But what, in any case, is the status of Crescas in (the history of) Western metaphysics? A Jewish philosopher born in Barcelona in 1340, he wrote in Hebrew, in a dialogue mainly with previous Jewish philosophers who mostly wrote in Arabic. Is Crescas too 'marginal' a figure to be considered at all, or is he to be placed 'outside' the history of philosophy from Parmenides to Husserl, aligned rather with a putatively 'non-western' history, perhaps a non-metaphysics, for which a non-Greek notion of time is not impossible — a possibility recently, apparently, suggested and even endorsed by Derrida in his citing of Chouraqui: ' "The Greek verb conceives time above all as a function of a past, a present, and a future: the Hebrew, or the Aramaic, on the contrary, instead of specifying the time of an action, describes its state under two modes: the finished and the unfinished. As Pedersen has seen so well, the Hebrew verb is essentially intemporal, that is, omnitemporal. I have tried, between two notions of time [*temps*] irreducible to one another, to resort most often to the present that in contemporary French usage is a very simple, very ample, very evocative tense [*temps*] . . ". '[5]

---

[3] Plotinus, *The Enneads*, trans. Stephen MacKenna, 4th. edition revised by B. S. Page, Faber & Faber, London, 1969, p. 228ff.

[4] Cf. H. A. Wolfson, *Crescas' Critique of Aristotle*, Harvard University Press, 1971, p. 269 and p. 651, note 23.

[5] Derrida, *D'un ton apocalyptique adopté naguère en philosophie*, Editions Galilée, Paris, 1983, p. 74n., trans. J. P. Leavey, *The Oxford Literary Review*, vol. 6, no. 2, 1984, pp. 36–37.

Yet, in that slide between differences of tense and irreducible notions of time, is Chouraqui merely rehearsing a deeply questionable eurocentric claim whose dubious genealogy is situated in close proximity to 1930s German anti-semitism and which has, *pace* Pedersen and despite its continued repetition by theologians and Biblical scholars, been devastatingly discredited by, among others, Barr and Momigliano?[6] Yet if, indeed, Hebraic notions of time are not a candidate for exemption from the systemic conceptual grip of 'Western' metaphysics, to what non-Western 'history of time' can Derrida appeal — Chinese, too, it seems, though once a fashionable ally, would hardly fit the bill.[7]

And if we return even to that most 'Aristotelian' of later Western metaphysicians, author of detailed *Commentaries* on both the *Metaphysics* and the *Physics*, St. Thomas Aquinas, there is a certain strained relationship with the Philosopher precisely at those points where Aristotle's arguments about time, change and action need to be reconciled with those assertions, problems, premises and concepts which St. Thomas derives not from (the history of) philosophy but from another text, another tradition, the Bible or dogmatic theology[8] — but does that double allegiance disqualify

---

[6] Cf. James Barr, *Biblical Words for Time*, SCM Press, London, 1962, and Arnoldo Momigliano, 'Time in Ancient Historiography', *History and Theory*, 6 (1966), pp. 1–23, reprinted in his *Essays in Ancient and Modern Historiography*, Blackwell, Oxford, 1977, pp. 179–204. Cf. also D. M. Mackinnon, 'Tillich, Frege, Kittel: Some Reflections on a Dark Theme', Explorations in Theology 5, SCM Press, London, 1979, pp. 129–37; R. P. Ericksen, 'Theologian in the Third Reich: the case of Gerhard Kittel', *Journal of Contemporary History*, 12 (1977), pp. 595–622; G. Kittel, *Die Judenfrage*, Stuttgart, 1933, and G. Kittel, ed., *Theologische Worterbuch zum neuen Testament*, Stuttgart, 1933.

[7] Cf. e.g. Joseph Needham, 'Time and Eastern Man', *The Grand Titration*, Allen & Unwin, London, 1969, pp. 218–98.

[8] Most obviously in Aquinas's various discussions of whether time and the world had a beginning; cf. *De aeternitate mundi contra murmurantes* (accessibly translated in Appendix 2 of *Summa Theologiae*, vol. 8, ed. Thomas Gilby, Eyre & Spottiswoode, London, 1967); and e.g. *Summa Theologiae*, Ia, q. 46; *Summa Contra Gentiles*, I, 13: 12, 13, 30; 15: 3, 6; 43: 13; 66: 7; II, 31–38; IV, 97. Cf. also Aquinas's discussions of the 'Real Presence' in the Eucharist and the problem of change in an instant (*Summa Theologiae*, IIIa, qq. 73–78), and the 'time' of angels (Ia, qq. 50–64). For Aquinas's own analysis of

Aquinas (and many others) from membership in 'metaphysics'? Indeed, are Derrida's claims as to the consistency and homogeneity of concepts of time to be sustained only by excluding from the 'history' of 'philosophy' such 'forgotten' authors as Crescas, Albo and Plotinus, such Christian theologians as Augustine or Scotus, such 'non-metaphysical' approaches as those of McTaggart, Wittgenstein or Mellor? Or, on the contrary, can — must — his claims be extended not only to all these texts but even to the ('metaphysical') 'grammar' underpinning the theories of time of, say, Newton, Einstein and Hawking?[9]

The question here is not simply whether a rigorous reading of all these texts, in a manner just as detailed as that of 'Ousia et Grammè' itself, would be needed to sustain the claims concerning 'history' in 'Ousia et Grammè', but also what relation any such readings *by Derrida* would, could, have precisely to 'Ousia et Grammè'. At stake is the problem not merely of agreeing or disagreeing with the results of Derrida's reading(s) but of their locus in a becoming, an itinerary or method, at the very least an order of reading, of Derrida.

Aristotle's argument on time, cf. *Commentary on Aristotle's Physics*, trans. R. J. Blackwell et al., RKP, London, 1963, Bk IV, Lectures 15–23, pp. 251–88.

[9] Cf. Augustine, *Confessions*, Bk. XI. 3ff and *City of God*, XI. 4, 6; XII, 11–16; for a useful discussion of Duns Scotus on time, see C. R. S. Harris, *Duns Scotus*, Oxford University Press, 1927, vol. II, ch. 4, pp. 122–46; J. M. E. McTaggart, *The Nature of Existence*, Cambridge University Press, 1927, vol. II, bk. V, ch. 33; D. H. Mellor, *Real Time*, Cambridge University Press, 1981. Wittgenstein's characteristic suggestion (*The Blue and Brown Books*, Blackwell, Oxford, 1964, p. 26) that Augustine's puzzlement about time could be resolved by clarifying the 'apparent contradictions' in the 'grammar' of time, can be usefully compared with Sarah Waterlow's analysis of the 'grammar' of Aristotle's arguments on 'change' and 'nature', in her *Nature, Change and Agency in Aristotle's Physics*, Clarendon Press, Oxford, 1982. For the notion of a 'metaphysical grammar' in relation to scientifi c theories, cf. Gerd Buchdahl, *Metaphysics and the Philosophy of Science*, Blackwell, Oxford, 1969.

There are two dates, at least, to be assigned to 'Ousia et Grammè', its appearance in *L'endurance de la pensée*, published by Plon in 1968, and a re-appearance in *Marges*, 1972. Among the differences between these two texts is a certain footnoted supplementation, a cross-referencing, in *Marges*, to other texts of Derrida: '*cf. plus loin*', to 'Form and Meaning', 'The Ends of Man', 'The supplement of copula', 'White Mythology', and, beyond Marges, to 'Double Session' in *Dissemination*. A familiar feature of an essay collection. Yet with Derrida a certain difference too, perhaps. A note in *L'écriture et la différence*:[10]

> Par la date de ces textes, nous voudrions marquer qu'à l'instant, pour les relier, de les relire, nous ne pouvons nous tenir à égale distance de chacun d'eux. Ce qui reste ici le déplacement d'une question forme certes un système. Par quelque couture interprétative, nous aurions su après coup le dessiner. Nous n'en avons rien laissé paraître que le pointillé, y ménageant ou y abandonnant ces blancs sans lesquels aucun texte jamais ne se propose comme tel. Si texte veut dire tissu, tous ces essais en ont obstinément defi ni la couture comme faufi lure. (Décembre 1966.)

An answer to an interview, 1967:

> One can take *Of Grammatology* as a long essay articulated in two parts . . into the middle of which one could staple *Writing and Difference* . . Inversely, one could insert *Of Grammatology* into the middle of *Writing and Difference* . . I could have bound [*Speech and Phenomena*] as a long note to one or other of the other two works.
>
> (*Positions*, p. 5)

---

[10] For an attempt to translate and gloss this dense paragraph, see Alan Bass, 'Translator's Introduction', *Writing and Difference*, RKP, London, 1978, p. xiii.

A comment, 'hors livre', referring to three essays dated 1966, 1970, 1969 'basted' in 1972, the year of publication of *Marges*:

> Dissemination produces (itself in) that: a cut/cup of pleasure. To be obtained in the break between the two parts of each of the three texts.
> (*Dissemination*, p. 57)

Are we, then, at liberty to cite across this chronology,[11] to treat this 'strange geometry' (*Positions*, p. 4) as 'flat and horizontal', these texts as contemporary, a co-present system ('*certes un système*'), simultaneous, or (*vel*) as stages in a development, a becoming? Either way, would we merely be falling into a 'vulgar concept' of time?

A public presentation (doubling as a whispered confidence, a confession), dated 2nd June 1980:[12]

> Never have I felt so young and at the same time so old. At the same time [*en même temps* ?], in the same instant and it is one and the same feeling, as if two stories and two times, two rhythms were engaged in a sort of altercation in one and the same feeling of oneself, in a sort of anachrony of oneself, anachrony in oneself.

*

---

[11] For example, to note that in 'Ousia et Grammè' Derrida writes of achieving a 'thought that henceforth may no longer need to be either true or present' (38), while in 'Plato's Pharmacy', also published in 1968 (*Tel Quel*, nos. 32, 33) he writes of 'the posture of the sophist; the man of non-presence and nontruth' (*Dissemination*, p. 66). Aquinas in his *Commentary* is content to characterise the 'exoteric' arguments at 218a as 'sophistical' (*Commentary*, p. 25).

[12] Derrida, 'The time of a thesis: punctuations', trans. Kathleen McLaughlin, in Alan Montefiore, ed., *Philosophy in France Today*, Cambridge University Press, 1983, p. 34.

'In short, is there a time of the thesis?'
(What is to paraphrase in philosophy?)

A system can, perhaps, be summarised, reduced, re-stated, re-assembled, re-presented, its reciprocal relations retained, recapitulated, its moments re-ordered towards structural simultaneity. But what of a text, a reading? 'Hegel himself has taught us that results are nothing without their becoming (*venir*)' (35). So, indeed:

> Nous devons en venir à la question du temps.
>
> A-t-elle encore à etre posée? A-t-on encore à se demander comment le temps apparaît à partir de cette genèse de l'espace? D'une certaine manière, il est toujours trop tard pour poser la question du temps. Celui-ci est déjà apparu. Le ne-plus-être et l'être-encore qui rapportaient la ligne au point et la surface a la ligne, cette négativité dans la structure de l'*Aufhebung* était déjà le temps. (*M* 47)

To write is, to begin with, once again, after all (as we say), to deploy points: *points finals* (full stops), *deux points* (colon), *point et virgule* (semi-colon), to *punct*-uate; to write in lines (*ligne d'écriture*), to begin a new paragraph (*aller à la ligne*), a new page (turn over a new leaf), be in the know (*être à la page*) or behind the times (*ne pas être à la page*). Even if, when, to make our extraordinary (*hors ligne*) point, we ask for reading between the lines, between the breaks, insert two texts in the middle of each other, re-arrange the lay-out, make up the page in double columns, re-order pagination, play with type-face, typography, line-spacing, different point type and spacing, our reader still has to *read*, in a certain *order* of reading, whatever order is in the end chosen.

What is in question is not only a matter of those temporally inflected indicators of order that most texts deploy ('Ousia et Grammè' not excepted: *un point de départ, jamais, à la fois, encore, jusqu'ici, passant à la . .* , still, if one considers now, yet at the same time, *il est toujours trop tard pour poser—passim*), or the peculiar practice of prefacing, or the relation between order of argument and order of presentation (cf. *Dissemination* on Marx, for example). What is in question is not only the time of thinking (a certain relation, for Jacques Lacan perhaps, between comprehension time and conclusion time), a time often allocated its own (a-) temporality in the history of metaphysics.[13]

What the matter comes down to, here, is reading time, constrained by a certain necessary non-simultaneity : faced with parallel columns, interlinear lay-out, we read, inescapably, it seems, according to a before and after, modifiable in any re-reading but always insistent. The reading eye(s) can only — it is how they are made — hesitate, go back, look across, down, up, follow the line (left to right, right to left), flip, scan, glance, one (part of the) text at a time. And yet, two normal, familiar devices subvert this linearity. First, the footnote, the superscription inviting a switch of attention, a suspension, an insertion.[14] The first six pages of 'Ousia et Grammè', in *Marges*, are divided almost equally, in terms of overall page-space, into 'text' and 'footnote'. Faced with a footnoted excursus on *Kant and the Problem of Metaphysics* or a reference (*plus loin*) to, say, 'Form and Meaning', do we suspend our reading of this text till we have read the footnote, even till we have read those 'later' essays, or perhaps even (re-)read the referred-to texts of Heidegger on Kant? We, probably, do not. But we do read or not-read text and footnote, reference or after-thought, in a certain order of interruption; we cannot follow both lines, read both at once, together, simultaneously (*hama*), even (especially) in 'Living On/Border Lines'.[15]

---

[13] Cf. Richard Sorabji, *Time, Creation and the Continuum: theories in antiquity and the early middle ages*, Duckworth, London, 1983, ch. 10, 'Myths about Non-Propositional Thought', pp. 137–56. Sorabji, incidentally, p. 10, suggests an Aristotelian solution to the aporia of 218a by appealing to *Metaphysics* 3.5, 1002a. 28–b. 11. Cf. also Jaakko Hintikka, Time and *Necessity: studies in Aristotle's theory of modality*, Clarendon Press, Oxford, 1973, ch. IV.

[14] Thus.

[15] Derrida, 'Living On/Border Lines', trans. James Hulbert, in Harold Bloom et al., *Deconstruction and Criticism*, Seabury Press, New York, 1969, pp. 75–176.

Yet on the seventh page Derrida begins quoting Heidegger's footnote, not in a footnote but as text, as quotation, noting that in *Being and Time* this footnote 'intervenes' 'at the end of the subsection devoted to the Hegelian exposition of the concept of time in the philosophy of nature' and 'before the subsection of "Hegel's Interpretation of the Connection between Time and Spirit".' (36). 'The Note,' writes Derrida, 'cuts this sequence in two.' A quotation is, it seems, precisely the possibility of reading 'two texts. . together simultaneously and separately' (65). A whole text, perhaps not in its own order, can be quoted in-as another text — a limit case (which 'Limited Inc.' approaches)[16] — or one text can be composed of quotations from other texts (themselves perhaps quoting quotations): 'You will be expected,' writes Derrida, in 'Dissemination', in *Dissemination*, 'to measure, to sum up, in a statistical accumulation of "quotations", the well-calculated, rhythmically regulated effects of a recurrence . . this accumulation will be the only means, not of presenting, but of feigning to present the text that, more than any other, writes and reads *itself*, presents its own reading, presents its own self-presentation, and constantly deducts this incessant operation. We will hence be inscribing — simultaneously — in the angles and corners of these *Numbers* [*Nombres*: title of a novel by Sollers], within them and outside them, . .certain questions that touch upon "this" text "here", the status of its relation to *Numbers*, what it pretends to add to "that" text in order to mime its presentation and re-presentation, in order to seem to be offering some sort of review or account of it. For if *Numbers* offers an account of itself, then "this" text — and all that touches it — is already or still "that" text.' And so forth. Thus: 'The duality between original text and quotation is thus swept away . . you have been warned: "1.5 . . *something had begun, but this beginning in turn revealed a deeper layer of beginning; there was no longer any before and after; it*

---

[16] Derrida, *Limited Inc.*, Johns Hopkins University Press, Baltimore, 1977, which quotes (the whole of) John Searle, 'Reiterating the Differences: A Reply to Derrida', from *Glyph*, no. 1.

was impossible to turn around . . — ".' (Dissemination, p. 294 and p. 335, quoting Sollers, *Nombres*).

Let us, then, turn back, at this point, to the pivot. 'The first phase of the alternative (none of the parts of time is — present — therefore time in its totality *is* not — which means "is not present", "does not participate in *ousia*") supposed that time was composed of parts, to wit, of nows (*nun*). It is this presupposition that the second phase of the alternative contests: the now is not a part, time is not composed of nows, the unity and the identity of the now are problematical.' (53) And Derrida follows his paraphrase of Aristotle's paraphrase of the traditional *aporia* with a partial quotation, here with its repressed phrase restored (italicised) again:

> If in fact the now is always other, and if none of the parts in time which are other are simultaneous (*hama*) — *except those of which one includes the other, as the greater time includes the smaller* — and if the 'now' which is not, but formerly was, must have ceased to be or been destroyed at a certain moment, the 'nows' too cannot be simultaneous (*hama*) with one another, but the preceding 'now' must always have been destroyed. 218a. (53–54)

Or, without indentation: "'If in fact . . destroyed." 218a.' The ' " " ' points, single and double, mark off, punctuate, the double quotation, frame the intra-citation, delimit the simultaneity of texts. (Derrida's own text continues: 'How do the concepts of *number* (as the numbered or the numbering) and of *gramme* [Greek: *grammē*, line, stroke of pen, etc; French: *gramme*, (measure) gram; Derridean: *grammè*, neologism] intervene in order to refurbish the same conceptuality in the same system?' — but let us postpone these further parentheses.)

The marks are separated by a space (' ") that marks off two nearly identical beginnings, two almost co-eval limits. But those marks are dispensable, as in 'Dissemination', 'silent' (we say) quotation. What, then, is the time of a quotation? Perhaps we should, now, after all, ask what the point is.

*

histesi he- dianoia : Thinking stands still with something

(Heidegger quoting Aristotle, *De Interpretatione* 16b 20)

. . time is that which erases time. But this erasure is a writing which gives time to be read...

(Derrida paraphrasing Hegel, *Phenomenology of Mind*)[17]

Is the final point of Derrida's note to pin-point the point at which Aristotle's analysis of time is already silently pre-determined by a pre-conceptualisation of time? Thus his citation of *hama* in 218a as the *cheville* of all Western metaphysics . . But in what sense, after all, is 218a Aristotle's text? At this point Aristotle is prefacing his own analysis of time by paraphrasing a traditional *aporia*, re-phrasing past formulations of apparently irresolvable problems: (a) whether time 'is', and (b) what the nature (*physis*) of time is. According to Derrida, Aristotle's failure to return to and answer the question of whether time 'is' is the evasion or omission that pivots metaphysics. But Aristotle's *order* of argument is important (and may not be the same as his order of presentation).[18] He indeed leaves problem (a) behind as an aporia; but his subsequent answer to problem (b) is such that no answer to problem (a), as formulated at 218a, is then called for, since the nature of time is argued to be such that

---

[17] Heidegger, *The Basic Problems of Phenomenology*, trans. Albert Hofstadter, Indiana University Press, Bloomington, 1982, p. 254; Derrida, *Marges*, p. 53n. Heidegger's *Die Grundprobleme der Phänomenologie*, which only appeared finally in 1975, is the text of a lecture course delivered in summer 1927, and in part fulfils the project outlined in the footnote upon which Derrida focusses; for Heidegger's own discussion of Aristotle on time cf. Pt. II, ch. l, sec. 19 (a).

[18] Cf. the analysis by Edward Hussey in his Introduction to *Aristotle's Physics Books III and IV*, Clarendon Press, Oxford, 1983, pp. xxxvi–xxxviii.

the very formulation of (a) becomes, is now recognisable as, inappropriate, inept, irrelevant. That *hama* figures in that now-abandoned paraphrastic formulation can hardly be held against Aristotle. Even so, Derrida *might* — if he would deign to show it — be right in reproving the whole subsequent history of metaphysics for an illicitly pre-determined metaphysics of time; but he would, on this evidence, at this point, have to exempt Aristotle himself from his charge. Yet at another point Aristotle's 'own' text does indeed seem vulnerable — precisely at that point where Derrida locates an 'anticipation' of Kant.

'The paradox would be the following: the originality of the Kantian breakthrough . . transgresses the vulgar concept of time only by making explicit something hinted at in *Physics* IV' (49–50) since 'In effect, *as Aristotle says,* it is because time does not belong to beings . . and because time is not of . . being in general, that it must be made into a *pure* form of sensibility (the nonsensuous sensuous)' (48). 'In anticipating the concept of the nonsensuous sensuous, Aristotle furnishes the premises of a thought of time no longer dominated simply by the present (of beings given in the form of *Vorhandenheit* and *Gegenwärtigkeit*)' (49). But the paradox, in fact, is this: at the precise point in *Physics* IV cited by Derrida, what 'Aristotle says' is '*hama gar kinēseos aisthanometha kai chronou*' — 'for simultaneously (*hama*) we have the sensation of movement and time' (219a 4). On this occasion, Derrida chooses to translate: 'c'est *d'ensemble* que nous avons sensation du mouvement et du temps,' and to gloss, to paraphrase: '. . il semble alors qu'un certain temps se soit passé et du même coup, *d'ensemble* (*hama*), un certain mouvement semble s'être passé' (*M* 55). As a footnote earlier remarks: 'The following pages may be read as timid prologemona to a problem of translation' (33, note 6). But perhaps one can make too much of a tiny word, a mere difference of translation, an element of signification, a *d'ensemble* as opposed to an *en même temps* ?

68

On the other hand, if the whole weight of Aristotle's text comes down upon *hama*, it is as well to recognise not only that, as Derrida does indeed note, '*Ama* veut dire en grec "ensemble", "tout à la fois", tous deux ensemble, "en même temps". Cette locution n'est d'abord ni spatiale ni temporelle' (*M* 64), but also that Aristotle explicitly defines his own use of *hama* (and several related terms) in *Physics* V.3 (226b 21) — a passage Derrida does not note: 'Things are said to be together (*hama*) in place when the immediate and proper place of each is identical with that of the other.' But to pursue this definition of *hama* in place and its relation to time would take us to parts of the *Physics* that Derrida's analysis does not reach — to the discussions of 'place', 'contact' and points, and the various uses of *hama*, in, for example, 209a, 212a, or in *Metaphysics* I, 9 and V, 6 — just as any discussion of the (simultaneous) perception or sensation of change and time 'together' would have to take into account, for example, passages in *De Anima* II, 6 and III, 1, *De Sensu*, I, 437a, *De Memoria* I, 449b–450a, II, 452b–453a, etc., etc.

The connections between *hama*, time, place, point and change are indeed difficult ('among the most difficult and decisive of the history of philosophy') but would require analysis precisely because Aristotle uses spatial change as an analogue, and more than analogue, of time. Analogue only, because (*pace* Derrida) time is related not just to spatial motion but to any form of motion or change (*kinēsis*); more than analogue because some moves in Aristotle's argument undoubtedly, and questionably, appeal to specific features of spatial motion.[19]

---

[19] Cf. e.g. G. E. L. Owen, 'Aristotle on Time', in *Motion and Time, Space and Matter: Interrelations in the History of Philosophy and Science*, eds P. Machamer and R. Turnbull, Ohio State University Press, 1976, and reprinted in *Articles on Aristotle 3: Metaphysics*, eds J. Barnes, M. Schofield, and R. Sorabji, Duckworth, London, 1979, pp. 140–56; cf. also Hintikka, *Time and Necessity*, ch. VI, pp. 114–34.

But the main point is that Aristotle's eventual definition of time, his answer to problem (b) — the *physis* of time — that time is the number of motion according to/by/in relation to (*kata*) the before and after (*ho chronos arithmos esti kinēseos kata to proteron kai husteron,* 220a 25)[20] designates 'time' as a predicate, even a predicate of a predicate, a category of a category, i.e. precisely as *not* having the kind of being of independent substantiality (*ousia*).[21]

To risk, indeed to appropriate, a paraphrase:[22]

> There is nothing more to time than that it is a measurable quantity which attaches to changes in just the same sort of way as e.g. length and heaviness attach to material bodies. There is, in particular, no unified, all-embracing self-subsistent 'Time': there are just changes having greater or lesser quantities of time-length.

Perhaps only a full and (I suppose) 'rigorous' reading of the whole of *Physics* IV, together with, at least, a consideration of Aristotle's treatment elsewhere of quantities and measurement (e.g. *Metaphysics* X. I, 1052b 14ff; *Metaphysics*, V. 13; *Categories* 6; *Physics* IV. 12, 220b 14ff) and his discussion of 'uniform' motion (*De Caelo* 11.6, *Physics* VIII. 10, V. 4), could justify, sustain this paraphrase, but — since Derrida equally does not provide such a reading — one can nevertheless say that in the light of that definition at 220a

---

[20] It is well worth consulting Liddell and Scott for the various possible senses here of *kata*.

[21] Cf. e.g. Franz Brentano, *On the Several Senses of Being in Aristotle,* trans. Rolf George, University of California Press, Berkeley, 1975 (originally published in 1862). Heidegger, it will be recalled, wrote: 'The first philosophical text through which I worked my way, again and again from 1907 on, was Franz Brentano's *Von der mannigfachen Bedeutung des Seienden nach Aristoteles,*' — see his Preface to W. J. Richardson, *Heidegger,* The Hague, 1963, p. xi. For Brentano's own views on time, and a critique of Heidegger's editing of Husserl's comments on Brentano in *The Phenomenology of Internal Time-Consciousness,* cf. Oscar Kraus, 'Towards a Phenomenognosy of Time Consciousness', translated in Linda McAlister, *The Philosophy of Brentano,* Duckworth, London, 1976, pp. 224–39. Kraus's article originally appeared in 1930.

[22] Hussey, *Aristotle's Physics Books III and IV,* Introduction, p. xxxviii.

there is no need for Aristotle to return to the first aporia of 218a since the kind of 'being' postulated of 'time' in *that* formulation is *not* the kind which characterises time.

Nor is it really necessary for Aristotle to return to the second aporia, concerning the part and the *nun*, since his subsequent analysis deploys '*nun*' not as 'part' but as 'limit', 'boundary' (as, in fact, Hegel, Heidegger and Derrida all recognise) and the conflation of 'now' with 'part' in 218a 10f renders the formulation there, and therefore the proposed aporia, inept. But though a complete commentary or even overall summary is precluded here (as it is for Derrida: his 'Note' is no more a *commentary* on Aristotle than it is an analysis of the *history* of philosophy . .), it is worth suggesting, playing with (it can be no more than that) a certain other analogue.

*

If one were to ask what is the (*physis*) nature and mode of being of a *quotation*, it is apparent that a quotation has to be a quotation *of* —a quotation depends for its kind of existence upon a relationship between at least two texts, that which is quoted (from) and that which quotes. (A single text could not be a quotation.) And it is the quotation marks, the ' ' or " " which, normally, mark off the 'end', the limit, boundary, of one text and the 'beginning' of another, though — *since the greater can include the lesser* — either beginnings or endings may coincide though not both together ("this" text consisting entirely of one quotation would be, in a sense, "that" text quoted): my text may begin (or end) with a quotation from Derrida's text, which may be the beginning (or ending) of his text. We use, for a certain convenience, marks which are neither indispensable nor *part* of the quotation (they mark it *as* a quotation but are not themselves quoted or from the text quoted) and we can indeed recognise a quotation without those boundary-signs; a spacing or indentation can substitute — a matter of conventions.

If we were to ask how many quotations a text includes we might seek to use such marks as indicative, merely counting the quotation marks themselves (the minimum unit would be two).[23] An unreliable procedure in practice, of course. But there is another question that might be asked: how much of a text consists of quotations? To answer that, a numerical count even of 'reliable' quotation marks (and some ' ' are not even marks of quotation)[24] is not enough, since even in the most statistical accumulation of quotations (see *Nombres*), quotation marks might not divide the text at sufficiently regular intervals to yield a unit of numeration we would accept; we would need to agree upon some other standard, a unit or uniform regularity. And that could be decided upon by reference to some (abstractly, ideally) uniform material feature of a text — the printer's **m** as a unit of line space, for example, or more simply a calculation in terms of page space (*Marges* pp. 33–38: 18 inches of text, 17 inches of footnote).

But of course a ' can interrupt the text to be quoted at any point: I can begin quoting from 'But..., from 'of course..., from 'can interrupt..., even from a ' itself — though in normal printing practice we deploy an after as well as a before: a single " or a " indicates before/after the beginning (or ending) of a quotation, but most quotations both open and close. The relations between this potentially intervening ', operating a before/after at variable points 'in' the text quoted from, and the metric of, for example, **m**-spaces (in either text) could be further explored, in a certain parallel reading with *Physics* IV on the relations between *nun* as limit, boundary, the point and the line (...), and materially regular motion (a matter, literally, of physics)—but it would be

---

[23] Cf. Derrida's original epigraph to section V ('The Pivot of Essence') of 'Ousia et Grammè', excised in *Marges*: 'The smallest number, strictly speaking, is two' (*Physics*, 220a).

[24] Cf. Derrida's remark, in *Éperons* p. 107, on 'the epochal regime of quotation marks which is to be enforced for every concept belonging to the system of philosophical decidability.'

tedious to develop a foredoomed analogy to the full. And, in that regard, point-less. Except to make a point, a limited but important point: a matter of de-mystification.

For, to quote, again, a paraphrase (Hussey's):

> Aristotle is *inter alia* trying to show that there is nothing intrinsically mysterious about time-stretches: all their inner structure is, as it were, borrowed from other, quite unmysterious things like spatially extended bodies, and they in themselves are straightforward, unstructured abstractions. The de-mystification of time is one of Aristotle's aims, and that perhaps is the reason why he spends relatively so much time on the description of (e.g.) time-measurement, and on the derivability of its properties. (p. xliii)

This is not to say that he succeeds, but one can suggest (neither a result nor a method, merely an itinerary) that a history of the concept of time might well be written which would prioritise, say, Augustine's recognition that 'time depends on motion and change, and is measured by the longer and shorter intervals by which things that cannot happen simultaneously succeed one another',[25] the related arguments of Leibniz (against Newton's — novel, innovative — notion of absolute time) that 'instants apart from things are nothings . . they only consist in the successive order of things' and 'the natural forces of bodies are all subject to mechanical laws . . (which) follow the order of efficient causes',[26] through to Albert Einstein's recognition that the constant velocity of light, which operates as the 'uniform motion' of relativity theory, is to be

---

[25] Augustine, *City of God*, trans. H. Bettenson, Penguin, Harmondsworth, 1984, p. 435; cf. also p. 491. One might consider, for example, that the same person being old and being young 'cannot happen simultaneously' (*pace* Derrida's feelings, cf. note 12 above); a certain concept of causality, and of history, is here, however, involved.

[26] From the correspondence with Clarke, in *The Philosophical Writings of Leibniz*, trans. M. Morris, Dent, London, 1934, pp. 200, 229.

defined (reciprocally) in terms, eventually, of a ratio between energy and mass, and then, further, to the more recent recognition that space-time results from a point singularity of massed energy.[27]

To put the point in this way is not, of course, to dissolve the problems tackled by Aristotle — they receive a re-formulation perhaps,[28] but it is to tackle them in the same *kind* of way as Aristotle. And, arguably, that way is, precisely, *a*- or *non*-metaphysical, a matter — as Aristotle said— of physics.

On this reading, it is the persistence of another, unnecessary, subordinate and intermittent component in Aristotle's analysis that would lead us in a different direct line (*un ligne direct*, says Derrida) from Parmenides to Husserl to Heidegger even to Derrida:

---

[27] Cf. e.g. A. Einstein, *Relativity*, Methuen, London, 1920. For attempts to situate the theory of relativity within a history, cf. Stanley Goldberg, *Understanding Relativity: origin and impact of a scientific revolution*, Birkhauser, Boston, 1984, and Lloyd S. Swenson, *Genesis of Relativity*, Burt Franklin, New York, 1979. For more recent developments, cf. W. J. Kaufmann, *The Cosmic Frontiers of General Relativity*, Little Brown & Co., New York, 1977, and G. W. Gibbons, S. W. Hawking, S. T. C. Siklos, *The Very Early Universe; Proceedings of the Nuffield Workshop, 1982*, Cambridge University Press, 1985. For an intriguing attempt to develop a theory of integrated levels of different times, see J. T. Fraser, *The Genesis and Evolution of Time*, Harvester, Brighton, 1982, which argues that since 'time is a symptom or correlate of the structural and functional complexity of matter' it follows that 'time itself has evolved with the increasing complexification of natural systems' (p. 1) — an approach that might have endeared itself to Aristotle. However, some important components of the dominant cosmological theory are again in question, cf. e.g. J. Gribbin, 'Galaxy Red Shifts', *New Scientist*, 20 June 1985, p. 20f.

[28] For an 'exoteric' (non-technical) exposition of some of the conundra of the new astrophysics, see John D. Barrow and Joseph Silk, The Left Hand of Creation: the origin and evolution of the expanding universe, William Heinemann, London, 1984, especially ch. 6. One might, e.g., compare the problem of 'left-handed' electron spin with Leibniz's question 'why everything was not put the other way round (for instance) by changing east and west'.

Besides that of the instant, there is another notion for which Aristotle wishes to make room: that of the present. The notion of the present had had a prehistory in Parmenides, Zeno and Plato's *Parmenides* [151e 3–152d 4] . . Aristotle justifies this notion of a persistent present by reference to his analogy with spatial magnitudes and change. But the analogy does not require the existence of any such thing . . and in accepting the existence of a persistent present Aristotle complicates his theory considerably. The fact must be that Aristotle thinks he has to accept the notion of a permanent present as given in the phenomenology of the subject. The notion does no further work within Aristotle's system. (Hussey, p. xliv)

Which is where Derrida would of course disagree, as he would disagree with the very notion of 'subordinate'. But to incorporate *Physics* IV within that metaphysical line as its pivot would require a different kind of analysis, a different focus upon Aristotle's text than that provided by *hama* in 218a, upon which 'Ousia et Grammè' rests its case.

Which is not, in fact, to say that one disagrees with certain of Derrida's conclusions or results, only with his reading of Aristotle's text. One could contest, say, the reading Derrida offers of Aristotle's argument concerning the point and the *nun* (especially the role in Aristotle's analysis of the moving body itself considered *as*, for this move only, a point) yet perhaps agree with his assessment of Heidegger's *Being and Time* as hinged upon a still-metaphysical opposition between 'the authentic and the inauthentic', primordial and fallen temporality (63), or with his analysis of the difficulty, perhaps 'impossibility', of distinguishing rigorously in Heidegger's text between 'presence as *Anwesenheit* and presence as *Gegenwärtigkeit*' (64). But insofar as 'all this, in sum' is 'in order to suggest' (63) — for example — that:

In order to exceed metaphysics it is necessary that a trace be inscribed within the text of metaphysics, a trace that continues to signal not in the direction of another presence, or another form of presence, but in the direction of an entirely other text (65)

—then one might suggest that Derrida should indeed have found some entirely other text than *Physics* IV, some other pivot (or trace) than *hama*.

Yet, of course, a word, even a concept, is not to be identified with, or opposed to, Derrida's 'trace':

The mode of inscription of such a trace in the text of metaphysics is so unthinkable that it must be described as an erasure of the trace itself. The trace is produced as its own erasure. And it belongs to the trace to erase itself, to elude that which might maintain it in presence. The trace is neither perceptible nor imperceptible. (65)

The *hama*, after all, was merely 'hardly visible' and 'self effacing' (56). But, of course, 'At the same time (*en même temps*) this erasure (*effacement*) of the trace must have been traced in the metaphysical text . . only on this condition can metaphysics and our language signal in the direction of (*faire signe vers*) their own transgression. And this is why it is not contradictory to think together (*ensemble*) the erased and the traced of the trace' (66; cf. *M* 76–77). (It is at this point that a footnote troubles the text, as Plotinus joins the *ensemble* of Derrida's texts....)

In the penultimate paragraph of his essay Derrida signals that wished-for direction, makes a sign (up):

There may be a difference still more unthought than the difference between Being and beings. We certainly can go further forward toward naming it in our language. Beyond Being and beings, this difference, ceaselessly differing from and deferring (itself), would trace (itself)

76

(by itself) — this *différance* would be the first or last trace if one could still speak, here, of origin and end. (67)

In an 'Address given before the *Société française de philosophie*, 27 January 1968, published simul-taneously [*sic*] in the *Bulletin de la société française de philosophie*, July–Sept 1968, and in *Theorie d'ensemble*, Coll. Tel Quel (Paris, . . 1968)' (1) — an address republished in *Marges* as 'Différance' — Derrida speaks (spoke; writes; wrote) of how this 'neographism' 'came to be formulated in the course of a written investigation of a question about writing' (3).

One would need to know the chronology of writing (if such there is) to know if this was indeed the penultimate paragraph of 'Ousia et Grammè' but perhaps a certain near-simultaneity is more relevant. In an essay, published in June–July 1963 but re-published as the opening essay of *L'écriture et la différence* (published in 1967), and already quoted from, 'Form and signification', Derrida had written:

> Since we take nourishment from the fecundity of structuralism, it is too soon to dispel our dream. We must muse upon what it *might* signify from within it. In the future it will be interpreted, perhaps, as a relaxation, (*détente*), if not a lapse, of the attention given to *force*, which is the tension of force itself. *Form* fascinates when one no longer has the force to understand force from within itself. That is, to create.
> (*Writing and Difference*, pp. 4–5)

Paris 1968, and precisely those months that cover the addresses, articles, essays, that make up much of *Marges*,[29] perhaps marked a point at which (from the future, now) one can locate a certain *détente*, a relaxation, if not a lapse, of the attention given to *force*, an emerging fascination for when

---

[29] The dates assigned to pieces in *Marges* include 16 January; 27 January; 3–4 February; 12 May; October — all from 1968; others date from August, November, December 1971 and May 1972.

one no longer had the force to understand (comprehend, include) force '*en son dedans*'.

The *form* of 'Ousia et Grammè' repays attention — not merely the itinerary, the method. A note upon a footnote, a note made up, in large part, of quotations (of paraphrases, too) from other texts, from Heidegger on Hegel on Aristotle on— ; made up, too, in considerable part, of its own footnotes, referring, often programmatically, to other texts, to other readings, to other possible writings:

> Here, we can only cite and situate several texts on which our examination would have to bear down, patiently.
>   (45, note 21)

> Again under the rubric of a preliminary survey, let us be satisfied, here, with translating Hegel's text . .
>   (46, note 22)

> One could show how this value of proximity and of self-presence intervenes, at the beginning of *Sein und Zeit* and elsewhere. . .
>   (64, note 39)

> That it does not go without saying is a problem that we cannot tackle here. We may refer, on the one hand, to . .
>   (51, note 31)

And dare one cite, at this point, another footnote, to a passage which speaks of the 'necessity' of a '*formal* rule for anyone wishing to *read* the texts of the history of metaphysics':

> Only such a reading, on the condition that it does not give authority to the security or structural closing off of questions, appears to us capable of undoing *today*, in *France*, a profound complicity: the complicity which gathers together (*rassemble*), in the same refusal to read, in the same denegation of the question, of the text, and

of the question of the text, in the same re-editions, or in the same blind silence, the camp of Heideggerian devotion and the camp of anti-Heideggerianism. Here, political "resistance" often serves as a highly moral alibi for a "resistance" of an other order: *philosophical* resistance, for example, but there are other resistances whose political implications, although more distant, are no less determined. (62, note 37)

What, then, is (has-been?) the fascination of this form, this itinerary, this way of coming? After 1968, a project has emerged, to deconstruct (so it is said) the whole of Western metaphysics — 'an enormous task is proposed here' — a valiant mission, extraordinary undertaking, undermining; a task of decisive, not marginal, significance, particularly insofar as violence, the force of totality, of totalitarianism, and metaphysics have already been recognised and delineated in their complicity.[30] What, in theory, in practice, was to be involved in this project? As of December 1967 what is to be our position?

> You know, in fact, that above all it is necessary to read and reread those in whose wake I write. . .
> (*Positions*, p. 4)

> To be entangled in hundreds of pages of a writing simultaneously *[sic]* insistent and elliptical, imprint-ing, as you saw, even its erasures, carrying off each concept into an interminable chain of differences, surrounding or confusing itself with so many precautions, references, notes, citations, collages, supplements . .
> (*Positions*, p. 14)

An enormous amount, quite (one might say) literally, of *reading time* is going to be required of us. To read, and re-

---

[30] Cf. Derrida, 'Violence et metaphysique: Essai sur la pensée d'Emmanuel Levinas', Revue de metaphysique et de morale, 1964, nos. 3, 4. Republished in L'écriture et la difference, 1967. The essay appears to date from mid- 1963.

read, and *re*-reread, these most difficult (and decisive) texts with such rigour, such intensity of attention (refusing even paraphrase) that not a single word, even a tiny self-effacing, hardly visible word like *hama*, or perhaps even a trace still less perceptible, will escape our reading. A truly enormous task. Almost a sanctified one. Yet, in its way, necessarily an endlessly deferred task, asymptotically undertaken, interminably recommenced; a displacement of a question that is never, will never be, a system of opposition, a systematic opposition (such terms are under erasure):

> All these texts, which are doubtless the interminable preface to another text that one day I would like to have the force to write, or still the epigraph to another that I would never have the audacity to write. . .
> (*Positions*, p. 5)

That moment, that position, for Derrida, may have passed. But the fascination remains: to take on not just (simultaneously, at a certain moment of crisis) *les flics*, the universities, de Gaulle, French capitalism, US imperialism, but (think of it!): Aristotle, Hegel, Kant, Heidegger, the whole of Western metaphysics, the entire history of philosophy from Parmenides to Husserl — and yet, in practice (for criticism of all these texts cannot be simultaneous) to read and write in an interminable deferral, '*un jeu de la soumission*' (M 72), a *deference*, a postponement, a supineness. At least, as always, it will keep us off the streets. (*"Sous les pavés, l'apostille!"*?)

Yet, in tracing the concept of time, for example, is there not, perhaps, an interesting omission (or evasion) thus far, to be rectified, returned to, a project of re-reading yet (again) to be undertaken? Among the most difficult, and decisive, of texts upon time is, was, a certain analysis of labour-time, indeed of socially necessary labour-time, not endowed with a metaphysical substantiality of its own, but as a predicate, a mode of numeration, of accounting (for), of *matériel*, of material processes of change, of production, perhaps a non-metaphysical (for that would be the question) resumption of an Aristotelian analysis of 'the general system of this economy' ('Differance' p. 3)?

And — on the other hand — in the insistent recognition of the 'repeatability of the sign', a 'repeatability' to be located not as some homogenous medium in which writing occurs, but as a determinate of the material character of inscription, is there perhaps, still (again), a danger (a trace) of a certain appeal (for that would be the question) to a meta-physical concept of time, already silently pre-determining the very notion of repeatability, a time abstracted from the always contextualised act of inscribing (*hama* does indeed occur five times in 218a)?

If indeed we are to 'think a writing without history, without cause, . . a writing that absolutely upsets all dialectics, all theology, all teleology, all ontology' (the final paragraph of 'Ousia et Grammè'), in re-inscribing those two Greek terms, *ousia* and *gramme*-, we might still do well to recall Heidegger's own gloss on the first:

> Disposable possessions and goods, property, are beings; they are quite simply that which is, the Greek *ousia*. In Aristotle's time, when it already had a firm terminological meaning philosophically and theoretically, this expression, *ousia*, was still synonymous with property, means, wealth. [31]

And a further sense of the second: *grammē*: the line across the course, to mark the starting or winning place. In a race, the line, the tape, by the very nature of its material and position, registers a decisive before-and-after, a marked

---

[31] Heidegger, *Basic Problems of Phenomenology*, p. 108. Heidegger had already, as it happens, anticipated Derrida in commenting on the (necessary but not necessarily tautologous) use of temporal terms in Aristotle's definition of time, cf. pp. 240f.

discrimination between winners and losers, first and second, an order of competitors.

To assert anything more than a certain simultaneity (always a matter of chance, coincidence, or causality) between the moment of "1968" (when history, perhaps, fell into time?) and the writing of 'Ousia et Grammè' would be to appeal to a perhaps as-yet unrethought notion of history, cause, change.[32]

But insofar as that history is not a mere homogenous medium within which intra- philosophical moments occur, the question we still cannot afford to displace, evade, omit or forget, is whether or in what way, in a general economy in which *ousia* and *gramme-*, wealth and competition, play no little part, our immense labour of reading-time is, still, socially necessary.

The Greeks had a phrase, used of the game of draughts: *ton apo grammēs kinein lithon*. It meant to move one's pieces off the crucial line; in other words: to try one's last chance, to risk one's final position in the game.

*

Whitstable, Kent, 4th – 5th July 1985*

---

[32] One might also — not quite at random — mention the almost simultaneous publication of the marxist historian E. P. Thompson's 'Time, work-discipline and industrial capitalism' in *Past & Present*, no. 38 (December 1967) pp. 56–97, and the situationist Guy Debord's *Société du Spectacle*, Paris, 1967, especially ch. V, 'Time and History', and ch. VI, 'Spectacular Time'. The revival of interest in relativity theory can, in part, be dated from the confirmation of pulsars in autumn 1967. Derrida may well be right that the problem of *hama*, of simultaneity, remains crucial to any re-conceptualisation of history and causality. I have offered some remarks on marxism and time in my 'Towards a Cultural Study of Time', forthcoming in David Punter, ed., *Introduction to Contemporary Cultural Studies*, Longmans, London, 1986, and in my *The Literary Labyrinth*, Harvester, Brighton, 1984, especially 'A Matter of Time', pp. 185–202.

* As the printed appearance of this contribution to the Derrida debate has presumably indicated, another essay could, and should, be written on the indispensable contribution to Derridean scholarship of the various editors, copy-editors, layout designers, estimators, typesetters, printers, and proofreaders, for whom Derrida's work must always have been a paranoia inducing nightmare. In this instance, I can only acknowledge my own debt to, especially, Rimina Mohapatra and her Routledge India colleagues. Any apparent typographical anomalies or oddities should be regarded by the reader as, deliberately, my own responsibility.

B.S. 5th November 2008

[I apologise to my Indian copy-editors for now, undoubtedly, having modified and thereby ruined their work.
B.S. May Day Bank Holiday, 2015.]

www.ingramcontent.com/pod-product-compliance
Lightning Source LLC
Chambersburg PA
CBHW070646030426
42337CB00020B/4181